Bloom's Modern Critical Interpretations

The Adventures of
Huckleberry Finn
The Age of Innocence
Alice's Adventures in
Wonderland
All Quiet on the
Western Front
Animal Farm
Antony and Cleopatra
The Awakening
The Ballad of the Sad
Café
Beloved
Beowulf
Black Boy
The Bluest Eye
The Canterbury Tales
Cat on a Hot Tin
Roof
Catch-22
The Catcher in the
Rye
The Chronicles of
Narnia
The Color Purple
Crime and
Punishment
The Crucible
Cry, the Beloved
Country
Darkness at Noon
Death of a Salesman
The Death of Artemio
Cruz
The Diary of Anne
Frank
Don Quixote
Emerson's Essays
Emma
Fahrenheit 451
A Farewell to Arms
Frankenstein
The Glass Menagerie

The Grapes of Wrath
Great Expectations
The Great Gatsby
Gulliver's Travels
Hamlet
Heart of Darkness
The House on Mango
Street
I Know Why the
Caged Bird Sings
The Iliad
Invisible Man
Jane Eyre
John Steinbeck's Short
Stories
The Joy Luck Club
Julius Caesar
The Jungle
King Lear
Long Day's Journey
into Night
Lord of the Flies
The Lord of the Rings
Love in the Time of
Cholera
Macbeth
The Man Without
Qualities
The Merchant of Venice
The Metamorphosis
A Midsummer Night's
Dream
Miss Lonelyhearts
Moby-Dick
My Ántonia
Native Son
Night
1984
The Odyssey
Oedipus Rex
The Old Man and the
Sea
On the Road

One Flew over the
Cuckoo's Nest
One Hundred Years of
Solitude
Othello
Persuasion
Portnoy's Complaint
Pride and Prejudice
Ragtime
The Red Badge of
Courage
Romeo and Juliet
The Rubáiyát of Omar
Khayyám
The Scarlet Letter
A Separate Peace
Silas Marner
Slaughterhouse-Five
Song of Solomon
The Sound and the
Fury
The Stranger
A Streetcar Named
Desire
Sula
The Sun Also Rises
The Tale of Genji
A Tale of Two Cities
The Tempest
"The Tell-Tale Heart"
and Other Stories
Their Eyes Were
Watching God
Things Fall Apart
The Things They
Carried
To Kill a Mockingbird
Ulysses
Waiting for Godot
The Waste Land
Wuthering Heights
Young Goodman
Brown

Bloom's Modern Critical Interpretations

Tim O'Brien's
The Things They Carried

Edited and with an introduction by
Harold Bloom
Sterling Professor of the Humanities
Yale University

BLOOM'S
LITERARY CRITICISM
An Infobase Learning Company

Bloom's Modern Critical Interpretations: The Things They Carried

Copyright © 2011 by Infobase Learning
Introduction © 2011 by Harold Bloom

Bloom's Literary Criticism
An imprint of Infobase Learning
132 West 31st Street
New York NY 10001

Library of Congress Cataloging-in-Publication Data
   Tim O'Brien's The things they carried / edited and with an introduction by Harold Bloom.
      p. cm. — (Bloom's modern critical interpretations)
   Includes bibliographical references and index.
   ISBN 978-1-60413-873-3
   1. O'Brien, Tim, 1946– Things they carried.   2. Vietnam War, 1961–1975—Literature and the war.   I. Bloom, Harold.   II. Title: Things they carried.
   PS3565.B75T4838 2011
   813'.54—dc22
                                        2010051341

Contributing editor: Pamela Loos
Cover design by Takeshi Takahashi
Composition by IBT Global, Troy NY
Cover printed by Yurchak Printing, Landisville, Pa.
Book printed and bound by Yurchak Printing, Landisville, Pa.
Date printed: April 2011
Printed in the United States of America

10 9 8 7 6 5 4 3 2 1

This book is printed on acid-free paper.

Contents

Editor's Note

My introduction acknowledges O'Brien's debt to Conrad, the Hemingway of *In Our Time*, and possibly the filmmaking of Francis Ford Coppola. Farrell O'Gorman opens the volume with a discussion of the book's metafictive formlessness, more arch perhaps than artful. Mats Tegmark then examines communication and multiple perspectives, particularly in the title story.

David R. Jarraway discusses the role of trauma in the literature associated with the Vietnam War, after which Jim Neilson considers the work's uneasy mixture of fact and fiction.

Carl S. Horner inevitably addresses notions of courage and heroism in O'Brien's work, followed by Christopher Michael McDonough's treatment of Homeric influence and the lingering shadow of another Asian conflict, the Trojan War, in the novel.

Pamela Smiley suggests that the soldiers perform their duties for the sake of the absent women so far removed from the realities of war. Susan Farrell also considers gender awareness and the role of the female auditor in the book's reliance on the restorative power of storytelling. In the volume's final essay, Alex Vernon examines the figuring of war as a means of attaining spiritual and personal salvation.

HAROLD BLOOM

Introduction

Rereading *The Things They Carried* (1990) has prompted me to reread also O'Brien's *Going After Cacciato* (1978). Initially I had read both at their time of publication and remember being more impressed by the earlier narrative. *The Things They Carried* came out of the era of "metafiction": the work of John Barth, Robert Coover, and others writing under the influence of the Argentine fabulist, Jorge Luis Borges, and the "magic realism" of Latin American fiction of "the Boom." Today, *Going After Cacciato* still seems to me a more adequate book than *The Things They Carried*, whose artful formlessness is arch rather than aesthetically gratifying. O'Brien's four books since essentially are repetitions, not so much variants on a theme but fainter echoes of our now faded national trauma, the Vietnam War syndrome.

Now, we are engaged in different quagmires, and doubtless we will suffer another trauma. I *want* to admire O'Brien's books more than I do, but they show all the stigmata of period pieces, which time will go on rubbing down, until the narratives vanish. Hemingway was always O'Brien's burden of literary anxiety. The narrative voice invariably is that of Nick Adams, itself indebted to Joseph Conrad's Marlow rather than to Mark Twain's Huck Finn, as Hemingway asserted. Perhaps by way of Francis Ford Coppola's *Apocalypse Now*, O'Brien also is dominated by *Heart of Darkness* as well as by Hemingway's *In Our Time*. This is reflected most dubiously by "Sweetheart of the Song Tra Bong," a wholly improbable tale of the metamorphosis of a seventeen-year-old American girl, Mary Anne, into a Green Beret killer. O'Brien is totally haunted by Marlon Brando's

1

countercultural Kurtz and asks us to accept the tall tale of an Ohio high
school girl who ends up as a blank-eyed ambusher, wearing a necklace
of human tongues. As a metaphor for American debasement in Vietnam,
this is too extravagant to be even minimally persuasive. It prompts me to
murmur Dr. Samuel Johnson's observation that only just representations of
general nature can endure.

FARRELL O'GORMAN

The Things They Carried *as Composite Novel*

I feel I'm experimenting all the time. But the difference is this: I am experimenting not for the joy of experimenting, but rather to explore meaning
and themes and dramatic discovery. . . . I don't enjoy tinkering for the joy
of tinkering, and I don't like reading books merely for their artifice. I want
to see things and explore moral issues when I read, not get hit over the
head by the tools of the trade.

(Anything Can Happen 269)

Novels have a kind of continuity of plot or of narrative which this book
does not have. But it would be unfair for me to say that it's a collection
of stories; clearly all of the stories are related and the characters reappear
and themes recur, and some of the stories refer back to others, and some
refer forwards. I've thought of it as a work of fiction that is neither one
nor the other.

(Missouri Review 96)

It would be more fun, it would be more instructive, it would be more artistic, more beautiful, to include as much as possible the whole of humanity
in these stories.

(Missouri Review 98)

From *War, Literature, and the Arts* 10, no. 2 (Fall–Winter 1998): 289–309. Copyright © 1998
by Farrell O'Gorman.

When Tim O'Brien's *If I Die in a Combat Zone* appeared in 1973, critics lauded the memoir and promptly prepared a place for the new author—three years out of Vietnam—in the ranks of the contemporary war writers who were trying to record what was happening in the bloody quagmire in which America, uncharacteristically, found itself mired. Such a characterization seemed borne out in his next two novels; both *Northern Lights* and *Going After Cacciato* were clearly representative of a new literature of the Vietnam experience. But in each of these works there is also ample evidence of his concern with issues broader than a specific war in Southeast Asia: indeed, even early readers recognized that *If I Die in a Combat Zone* was no mere raw emotional record of war experiences but rather "a spare, poetically allusive, and classically toned personal memoir" (Myers 141).

Such an observation suggests the true scope of O'Brien's interests: in his work there is an abiding concern with the question of battlefield courage, linking him with not only with the best of a tradition of American war writers—Cooper, Crane, Hemingway—but also with the ancients; a more general concern with moral choice and the human capacity for evil which links him to such writers as Conrad (perhaps his most oft-cited influence); and, finally, an explicit interest in storytelling itself, in narrative forms and the power of the imagination, which might connect him to a number of experimental writers, both modern and postmodern. Critics have gradually acknowledged this complexity, and O'Brien has accordingly gained increasing recognition as a writer concerned not only with that war Americans like to think of as so peculiar but also as one whose "fundamental themes . . . grant his work larger, even universal significance" (Myers 141).

O'Brien's own comments strongly support such readings of his work. In interviews he has cited as influences not only fellow Midwestern soldier-novelist Hemingway, but also Fitzgerald, Faulkner, and Joyce. Even more ambitiously, he has acknowledged that "the good writer must write beyond his moment, but he does have to be rooted in a lived-in world—like Conrad, Shakespeare and Homer" (qtd. in Myers 142). While his own "concerns as a human being and concerns as an artist have at some point intersected in Vietnam" (*Missouri Review* 101), those concerns are perennially human ones—with courage, moral choice, storytelling, "mysteriousness," and the experience of "awakening into a new world, something new and true, where someone is jolted out of a kind of complacency and forced to confront a new set of circumstances or a new self" (*Missouri Review* 99). O'Brien, then, rather traditionally sees the writer as communicating age-old themes that are newly manifested in his particular imaginative world; ultimately he sees his own subject matter as bounded not by the events of one war but rather by the full range of human experience itself.

The veracity of such a claim seems more apparent given O'Brien's broadened scope in his later novels, which are more generally about the American experience. *The Nuclear Age* (1986) is a parody about a nation obsessed with total war and apocalypse; *In the Lake of the Woods* (1994) concerns a husband and wife and the inevitable secrets of married life. But, ironically, it is perhaps in his 1990 publication of *The Things They Carried*—his first full-length return to the terrain of Vietnam in the twelve years since *Going After Cacciato*—that he most fully commits himself to exploring the universal concerns he speaks of so frequently in interviews. In fact, in *The Things They Carried* he is more consciously than ever before coming back to Vietnam with the intention of making it a story about the whole of human experience.

* * *

Thomas Myers has claimed with regard to *The Things They Carried* that "in a radically different way from his earlier combat zone narratives, the work depicts Vietnam as both 'this war' and 'any war'" (153). O'Brien would welcome such an observation, for he has maintained that, despite the general American perception of the war as an anomaly, Vietnam was not really an exception. In an interview with Larry McCaffery, he denies that his war was "especially chaotic and formless." He claims that the work of earlier writers—he mentions Siegfried Sassoon, Robert Graves, Rupert Brooke—has enabled him to acknowledge this fact most fully: "Every war seems formless to the men fighting it . . . We like to think our own war is special: especially horrible, especially insane, especially formless. But we need a more historical and compassionate perspective. We shouldn't minimize the suffering and sense of bewilderment of other people in other wars" (*Anything Can Happen* 267). Such a statement encapsulates O'Brien's own commitment to at once capture the unique fury of his own conflict and to communicate it to posterity as something eternally, horribly human.

What is surprising is that he does so most powerfully by moving beyond the battlefield. Readers of *The Things They Carried* are immediately struck by its variety of settings—which include not only the killing grounds of Vietnam, but also the small towns and cities of America—and the variety of characters to be found in these settings. Speaking specifically about his unusual choice to place a Midwestern American female in Vietnam in his story "Sweetheart of the Song Tra Bong," O'Brien claimed "it would be more fun, it would be more instructive, it would be more artistic, more beautiful, to include as much as possible the whole of humanity in these stories" (*Missouri Review* 98).

This claim is central to understanding the structure of the work as a whole. For more compelling than any discursive statement about the universal

nature of war, or any conventionally presented variety of setting and character, is O'Brien's unconventional choice of form in *The Things They Carried*.
Consisting of short stories published separately over nearly a decade, but
reworked, reordered, and bound together with various additions, the work
defies traditional generic distinctions. O'Brien himself has described it as
something of an anomaly:

> Novels have a kind of continuity of plot or of narrative which this
> book does not have. But it would be unfair for me to say that it's
> a collection of stories; clearly all of the stories are related and the
> characters reappear and themes recur, and some of the stories refer
> back to others, and some refer forwards. I've thought of it as a work
> of fiction that is neither one nor the other. (*Missouri Review* 96)

Why this particular form, then? O'Brien has always been distinguished
from more pedestrian "war writers" by his technical and stylistic skill, his ongoing interest in metafiction and in the surreal. Yet he was annoyed at having
Going After Cacciato characterized so strongly as a purely experimental work:

> I feel I'm experimenting all the time. But the difference is this: I
> am experimenting not for the joy of experimenting, but rather to
> explore meaning and themes and dramatic discovery.... I don't
> enjoy tinkering for the joy of tinkering, and I don't like reading
> books merely for their artifice. I want to see things and explore
> moral issues when I read, not get hit over the head by the tools of
> the trade. (*Anything Can Happen* 269)

Given this explicit attitude, one might infer that O'Brien has chosen or
"developed" this form—consciously or not—because it best serves his purpose here. O'Brien's narrator persona notes in "The Ghost Soldiers" that in
Vietnam "we were fighting forces that did not obey the laws of twentieth-
century science" (229); and it seems that in describing those forces, as well
as the universal forces of the human psyche, he felt compelled to move from
the established linear form of the novel to something more complex and
potentially richer. *The Things They Carried* is, accordingly, best characterized as
neither novel nor collection of short stories, but as what Maggie Dunn and
Ann Morris have recently defined as a composite novel. Their definition in
The Composite Novel: The Short Story Cycle in Transition describes this form as
the genre of connectedness: "the aesthetic of the composite novel" is such that
"its parts are named, identifiable, memorable; their *interrelationship* creates
the coherent whole text" (5–6). O'Brien, it seems clear, is using the composite

novel form not for artifice's sake but rather to "explore meaning and themes and dramatic discovery"; and he is writing not just a Vietnam story, not even just a war story (adapting Faulkner, he claims that "war stories aren't about war—they are about the human heart at war" [qtd. in Myers 142])—but rather a story and stories about the whole of humanity, and he has chosen the composite novel as the most appropriate form to do so.

He accomplishes this goal by using the strengths of the composite novel in its ability to link seemingly disparate stories by using some common, recurring focus(es). Here he develops to the full various latent possibilities of relationship in the composite novel: by using setting as a referential field that includes not only Vietnam but also middle America, linking the two together as a psychically united region; by using character in a similar sense, focusing on both a collective protagonist and an emerging narrator protagonist; by making storytelling, the process of fiction making itself, a recurring focus; and finally—in a strategy all his own—by using the composite novel's heightened possibilities for allusion to make his work part of a broader literary and human endeavor (and for all its alleged novelty, even this seemingly "new" composite novel form is ultimately linked with a tradition, a tradition which O'Brien is tapping into and thereby connecting his work with that larger "historical perspective" of which he spoke).

In O'Brien's return to Vietnam in *The Things They Carried*, then, he shifts to a new form in order to accomplish his broad goal most fully: the composite novel allows him to play with multiple settings, characters, the theme of storytelling, and even allusiveness, in a way that most fully incorporates "the whole of humanity" into his story. Here, using Morris and Dunn's concept as a framework and occasional guide, I want to briefly touch on all of these aspects of the work.

* * *

O'Brien has said explicitly that "my concerns as a human being and my concerns as an artist have at some point intersected in Vietnam—not just in the physical place, but in the spiritual and moral terrain of Vietnam" (*Missouri Review* 101). His vision of the war clearly seems to fall within Morris and Dunn's conception of the composite novel that employs setting as a referential field, thereby portraying place as not only "a specific geographical space" reflecting "a common ethos or culture," but also as "less concretely dependent upon physical space and more abstractly dependent upon a historical moment or period" (36).

With regard to the first characteristic, O'Brien's Vietnam is fully a locus *and* an ethos. Indeed, it is so much of an ethos that at times it seems almost a

ghost-place, a region of the psyche rather than of Southeast Asia. This characteristic is clear not only in explicit statements about the land being "haunted"
(in "The Ghost Soldiers," 229) and even *talking* . . . the fog too, and the grass
and the goddamn mongooses" (in "How to Tell a True War Story," 81), but
also in O'Brien's implicit sense of the cultural depth of the country; his sensitivity to the mysterious otherness of Vietnam, and the tragedy of America's
failure to recognize it, is revealed in such short vignettes as "Church," in the
personal history that makes "The Man I Killed" so poignant, and in the fitting
metaphor of the centuries-deep cultural quagmire the U.S. so blithely wades
into in "In the Field."

But O'Brien uses the structure of the composite novel to emphasize
more clearly the second characteristic, that which portrays place as less a
physical phenomenon and as more "abstractly" dependent upon a specific historical period. Implicit in his comment about the "moral terrain" of Vietnam
is the fact that this terrain necessarily includes the United States, for his moral
experience in that country was profoundly, definitively shaped by the fact that
he was there as an American soldier; the word "Vietnam" in his statement
encompasses not merely one place but also a time, an enduring moment in
our national history, one which spanned the seemingly insurmountable geographical boundary of the Pacific and linked two radically different countries
in one horrible experience (and O'Brien has insisted that he cannot write
about the war as anything but an American, cannot but superficially attempt
to portray what it was like for the Vietnamese people—"The Man I Killed"
may be as close as he comes to trying to do so). Today many Vietnamese
immigrants to this country rightly criticize Americans for still failing to recognize that their country is not a war, but a place; for O'Brien as for many
other veterans, however, it was and remains quite inseparably both.

The structure of the composite novel allows O'Brien to connect Vietnam and America more radically than he might have done in a "conventional"
novel, to depict artfully the radical connection of the seemingly disparate
countries. The first (and eponymous) story, "The Things They Carried," establishes this connection in its first sentence, which links First Lieutenant Jimmy
Cross to "Martha, a junior at Mount Sebastian College in New Jersey" (3).
The foxholes of Vietnam and this collegiate world in the urban American
Northeast are bound together inexorably, and the rest of the story—despite its
largely "factual" tone—will suggest that all of what these men carry through
this foreign place is ultimately attached to America, whether it be supplies
from "the great American war chest," "sparklers for the Fourth of July, colored
eggs for Easter" (16), or the bonds of emotion. And "Love," which follows
immediately after, suggests that the bonds run both ways through space, and
through time as well; set in Massachusetts, the story depicts Jimmy Cross

and O'Brien's narrator persona perhaps a quarter century later, remembering Vietnam by remembering the girl from New Jersey.

Similar connections are established regularly throughout the work, next—in another explicit act of remembrance—in "On the Rainy River," where the narrator persona leaps back in time from some indeterminate postwar present to the summer before his entry into Vietnam; before he tells any more about that bloody tropical place he must tell about small-town America and the placid, cold northern woodland that is the border of Minnesota and Canada. Having done so, he leaps back into vignettes set again in the war itself (though interspersed with more letters home; e.g., Rat Kiley's in "How To Tell a True War Story") before attempting what is perhaps his most radical connection of the two countries, in "Sweetheart of the Song Tra Bong." Almost midway through the book, this story goes further than any other in drawing America into this violent ghost-place, Vietnam. The war's seduction of Mary Anne Bell, a young girl fresh from Cleveland, bespeaks the fundamental involvement of even the most seemingly innocent Americans in this setting. After a few weeks in the country, she wants "to *eat* this place. Vietnam. I want to swallow the whole country . . ."; and by the story's end, she is in fact "part of the land. She was wearing her culottes, her pink sweater, and her necklace of human tongues" (125). Then, after O'Brien delves as closely as he might into the Vietnamese experience of the war in "The Man I Killed," he again shifts the next lengthy story in space and time, back to America and after the war. In "Speaking of Courage," Norman Bowker is the returned veteran living in the small town Midwest in the silent aftermath of Vietnam. The ennui of his life here seems diametrically opposed to the anxiety of life in the war; yet, once again, the two experiences are part of the same whole. The ennui of the war itself has been evident in other tales, and the drama of the war intrudes here—in Iowa—as he remembers the night of Kiowa's death. And throughout this story, the lake Bowker circles both serves as the centerpiece of his current mundane existence and suggests the horror of the boggy field, which is only gradually revealed to the reader.

Indeed, in this story and in "Notes," "In the Field," "Good Form," and "Field Trip," O'Brien reveals a single event through glimpses of Norman Bowker's life in 1975 Iowa, the murky "present" of the narrator persona in Massachusetts, the wartime past of Alpha Company, the narrator's Massachusetts present again, and then a few months more into that present—but back in Vietnam. These four adjacent stories, perhaps more comprehensively than any others, encapsulate the scope in space and time of the work as a whole. But then O'Brien, after briefly returning to the familiar (in "The Ghost Soldiers" and "Night Life," two more stories set in the conflict itself) performs his most drastic expansion of place and time at the very end of *The Things*

They Carried, in "The Lives of the Dead." Here the narrator persona begins by recording his first exposure to death in Vietnam, but uses this tale as an occasion to frame his very earliest experience of death. In doing so he returns again to his prewar Minnesota, but not to the time of "On the Rainy River"— no doubt just a few months prior to this incident—but rather to an utterly pre-Vietnam era, 1956, and his childhood. His first exposure to death on the battlefield becomes an occasion to reflect on the common human experience of death, whether it comes in a napalmed village in wartime Southeast Asia or in the movie theaters and shopping malls of the peacetime United States. O'Brien here uses a radical shift of setting to suggest finally a truth that transcends place, but only after he has masterfully used the composite novel to render the boundaries between America and Vietnam fluid, to merge both together as not just a "physical place" but also "spiritual and moral terrain," to depict aspects of the experience of a whole American generation, and—even more broadly—that of the whole of humanity.

* * *

The previous discussion of setting suggests another manner in which the collected stories in *The Things They Carried* unite to form a composite novel: through their development of both, on the one hand, a clear "collective pro-tagonist," and, on the other, an "emerging protagonist"—a narrator persona who is apparently Tim O'Brien but who is in fact, as the reader discovers, largely invented.

Morris and Dunn define the collective protagonist as "either a group that functions as a central character" or "an implied central character who func-tions as a metaphor (an aggregate figure who . . . may be . . . archetypal . . .)" (59). In this work the applicability of the first definition seems quite clear; the title, after all, is concerned with a "they" that seems quite clearly delineated in the dedication to the "men of Alpha Company." Yet given O'Brien's statement regarding the appropriateness of including women in the war in "Sweetheart of the Song Tra Bong" and the nature of the work itself, we might extend the concept of the collective protagonist even further. The composite novel struc-ture necessarily works against assigning any character a "minor" status, and, as we have seen in the previous examination of the complexities of setting, these stories are painfully inclusive of civilians as well as soldiers—indeed of as much of the whole of humanity as O'Brien can squeeze in. Therefore, not only Jimmy Cross, Norman Bowker, and Kiowa are central characters here, but also Martha, Elroy Berdahl, Mary Anne Bell, even Linda (the first and last names in this list—in the first and last stories—suggest that *The Things They Carried* is as much a story about love as it is about war).

Perhaps a similar observation might also be made regarding the development of a "single" archetypal protagonist here—something like the disillusioned veteran of Hemingway's *In Our Time*—but there is a clearer and more undeniable focus on a shifting persona who is a sort of Tim O'Brien. Morris and Dunn observe in many composite novels "a narrator-protagonist as the focus and significant element of interconnection" (49), and such is clearly the case in *The Things They Carried*. The author has confirmed in interviews what his narrator persona says at the beginning of "Good Form": that, other than the fact that he is a writer and a former foot soldier in Quang Nai province, "almost everything else is invented." Indeed, even as he writes this "I invent myself" (203).

While this ongoing invention serves to unite the various stories here, it might not necessarily entail any sort of positive progression. The narrator persona is a shadowy figure at best, one hard to pin down in space and time; he is perhaps more accessible in telling about himself in the past than he is in talking "bluntly"—as he says he will in "Good Form"—in the present. He is a figure who is at once seemingly honest and idealistic (his claim that "this is true" runs like a refrain throughout the work), but also cowardly—as in "On the Rainy River"—and crassly vengeful—as in "The Ghost Soldiers."

He is also a writer who gives credit to his sources, and in doing so reveals how even in developing this single protagonist O'Brien again bears witness to the experience of the whole of humanity. The work begins with "The Things They Carried," one of the few stories here told entirely in third person; there is no "I" or even "we" here. But immediately following, in "Love," Jimmy Cross—whose story has just been told—comes to visit "me" at home after the war and to tell another story about Martha. The narrator-protagonist has entered *The Things They Carried*, and will remain for almost the duration; but almost always he speaks in collaboration with other storytellers, such as Mitchell Sanders (whose tale is essential to "How to Tell a True War Story") and Rat Kiley (who relates the bulk of "Sweetheart of the Song Tra Bong" and others), even Norman Bowker. "Speaking of Courage" is in third person but is immediately followed by "Notes," which gives credit for the preceding story to Bowker; and this almost confessional story is in turn followed by a third and final third person narrative. "In the Field" shows the narrator—almost certainly—as a young, frightened "boy" (186) amidst a group of not much more secure men, including—once again—Lieutenant Jimmy Cross.

Indeed, this recurrently collaborative storytelling function almost implies an emerging *collective* narrator-protagonist, and suggests as much about O'Brien's concept of narrative as it does about his notions of character. It is noteworthy that in the text itself, in "The Man I Killed," O'Brien writes of his Vietnamese victim: "He knew he would fall dead and wake up in *the stories of his village and people* [emphasis added]" (144). O'Brien sees *The Things They Carried* as to a large extent the story of his own village and people, and so gives his characters their fair share in the telling. As he claims in his essay "The Magic Show," what the writer must do, like the shaman, is to summon "a collective dream" among his people (178).

In some sense, then, the emerging narrator-protagonist of *The Things They Carried* is radically inseparable from the collective protagonist; and yet in "The Lives of the Dead," the focus moves from the men of Alpha Company back to the individual narrator-protagonist Tim, to a quite personal story of his youth in Minnesota. Moreover, this final piece is equally a story about storytelling, about "Tim trying to save Timmy's life with a story" (273). As such it, along with the other complexities of narrative touched on above, suggests a third focus that unifies the work: storytelling itself.

* * *

Morris and Dunn claim that storytelling, "the process of fiction making" itself, can become a unifying focus in the composite novel (88); as the previous discussion of the narrator-protagonist indicates, in this metafiction such a process is clearly at the center of the narrative. Indeed, "How to Tell a True War Story" may have been an even more appropriate title story for the collection than "The Things They Carried"; not only it but also "Spin," "Ambush," "Notes," "Good Form," and "The Lives of the Dead" explicitly discuss this particular form of truth-telling, and all of the stories here do so implicitly.

O'Brien's explicit concern with talking about storytelling here, in fact, ultimately calls into question the extent to which he is making up stories at all. His metafiction confuses traditional genre distinctions, so that Dan Carpenter can suggest *The Things They Carried* "evokes the hyperintense personal journalism of Michael Herr and the journalism-as-novel of Norman Mailer," but is in fact both fiction and nonfiction, even "an epic prose poem of our time" (qtd. in Kaplan 190). O'Brien would certainly be pleased with any such suggestion that his work is, far from being merely "postmodern," in fact in the tradition of great modern—and even classical—writers. He has cited the influence of not only Faulkner and Joyce but even Homer in conveying to him the sense of "nonlinear time, the experience of one's life as jumps and starts" (Myers 144); and he has indicated his belief that the great stories are those that are continually "retold" and thereby "carry the force of legend" (156). Even Morris and Dunn speak of the composite novel as achieving the very effect of which O'Brien speaks, precisely by returning to the form of "the sacred composite, the epic cycle, and the framed collection." It is in fact this classical conception of storytelling—if his theme is that of the *Iliad*, his form is that of the *Odyssey*—which most fully allows O'Brien to unite his "Vietnam" stories with the whole human experience, not only with humans alive at this time and place in Vietnam and America, but all those living and dead.

O'Brien's notion of the writer-shaman summoning a "collective dream" suggests his view that storytelling itself is by nature communal. His entire collective-metafictional technique here is perhaps a way of getting at larger cultural and human truths. In Mitchell Sanders's tale about a "talking" Vietnam in "How to Tell a True War Story," in the tale of the man who "would fall dead and wake up in the stories of his village and people" (144) in "The Man I Killed," and in the generations-deep quagmire of "In the Field," it is clear that O'Brien senses something like an alien collective unconsciousness in Vietnam, a mysterious cultural psyche that is known—albeit only partially—through talk and stories. What he does with the new yet ancient form of the composite novel is to tap into some of the established myths of his *own* culture. In short, he alludes to older stories, stories which bespeak both his own tradition and the perennially human heart—and particularly those told in this century through the form of the composite novel. O'Brien's commitment to the stories of the past, to the dead as well as the living, is established by the beginning epigraph from a Civil War diary (also by a former sergeant from the Midwest, as Philip Beidler notes [37]). But his commitment to a small pantheon of great moderns can be established by briefly examining his allusions—both thematic and formal—to three writers for whom he has repeatedly expressed admiration: Conrad, Hemingway, and Joyce.

O'Brien has expressed his disappointment with the majority of films purporting to chronicle the war in which he served, but he admits an at least partial admiration for *Apocalypse Now*, which places a mad Colonel Kurtz at the end of a river deep in the jungles of Southeast Asia. The idea of enacting *Heart of Darkness* during the Vietnam conflict was, then, not a new one when O'Brien wrote "Sweetheart of the Song Tra Bong," but it certainly seems to be one he draws from with a power all his own. As noted previously, he has spoken repeatedly of Conrad's influence on his work, which is thematically evident throughout all of *The Things They Carried*. But it is concentrated in "Sweetheart" and with the brilliant adaptation of not only shifting the setting to Vietnam but also of characterizing the corruption of a Kurtz who is not a merchant or colonel, but rather an archetypally innocent American female. Although *Heart of Darkness* is obviously not drawn from a composite novel itself, the composite novel form allows O'Brien to—in the middle of a "longer" work—echo one of the greatest works of twentieth-century short fiction.

Carpenter referred to *The Things They Carried* as "an epic prose poem of our time," but doubtlessly O'Brien also had in mind one of the great

American composite "war" novels of our era: *In Our Time*. The newer work parallels Hemingway's account of the generation that fought the first great war of this century both in its overall form and in individual stories. "Speaking of Courage," featuring a tired veteran returned to his small Midwestern town, almost certainly echoes Hemingway; as Steven Kaplan notes, "Norman Bowker's dilemma is . . . remarkably similar to that of Hemingway's character Krebs in the story 'Soldier's Home.' Neither of these men returning from war can tell his story" (189).

Yet while both here and throughout the work O'Brien follows his great predecessor in searching for a definition of courage, he "asserted early in his career that his conclusion could not be a mere restatement of Hemingway" (Myers 144). In his novel *Northern Lights*, for example, there are some forty pages of parody which echo *The Sun Also Rises* (much to the dismay of critics); and while *The Things They Carried* is, fortunately, tainted by nothing so distracting, it is not impossible that O'Brien is reacting to Hemingway even in "On the Rainy River." O'Brien has stated that the story is a dramatization of the "moral schizophrenia" he felt during the summer of 1968, but that its plot and setting are entirely invented. He saw the river as a concrete means of putting his character "on the edge" (*Missouri Review* 95–6); but it is also difficult to read the story, set in the woods of the northern Midwest and climaxing in a fateful fishing trip, without thinking of "Big Two-Hearted River." The loquacity of O'Brien's narrator persona here, however, could not be further removed from the reticence of Nick Adams and his creator; and his open-hearted, anguished concern about the war is emotionally at opposite poles from the ideal of "grace under pressure."

Though he may call Hemingway's ideals into question in "On the Rainy River," O'Brien ultimately emulates the great example of *In Our Time* in this story, in "Speaking of Courage," and in his utilization of the very form of the composite novel. Given the parallels between his theme and that of Hemingway, his choice to do so is hardly surprising; the imaginative leap from World War I to the Vietnam conflict was perhaps even less difficult to make than that from the jungles of Africa to those of Southeast Asia. But in his final story O'Brien moves from his concern with moral corruption and war to one even more universally human: death. In doing so he sets in 1956 Minnesota a brief tale that alludes to another tale in the most surprisingly alien setting yet—turn-of-the-century Ireland. At the close of *The Things They Carried*, O'Brien establishes a connection to another of the great composite novels of the twentieth century, Joyce's *Dubliners*.

Like Joyce's "The Dead," O'Brien's "The Lives of the Dead" comes at the end of his work and establishes the ongoing presence of the dead in the lives of the living. An individual death in wartime Vietnam, which introduces the story, is linked in the narrator persona's mind with the death of a young girl in his childhood, in peacetime Minnesota. O'Brien's story, like Joyce's, is one which is about both death and first love, and suggests that the two are necessarily bound together; just as for Gretta Conroy the love of Michael Furey is bound up with his death, so too the narrator Tim O'Brien cannot think long of death without thinking of his innocent love for lost Linda. Both stories also suggest that what O'Brien called the "whole of humanity" somehow includes "all the living *and the dead* [emphasis added]," as Joyce would say; and the contemporary writer knows that the ranks of "the dead" now include Joyce himself. O'Brien's allusiveness to *Dubliners*, to "The Dead" and the literary tradition Joyce helped to establish, bears witness to this conviction.

And, fittingly, in this last story O'Brien concludes *The Things They Carried* not only by shifting settings and bringing in the character of Linda (who has perhaps been with the narrator all along), not only by once again alluding to the broad literary tradition he seeks to emulate, but also by presenting his strongest vision of storytelling itself. In his essay "The Magic Show" he has discursively suggested something of this vision:

> The process of imaginative knowing does not depend upon the scientific method. Fictional characters are not constructed of flesh and blood, but rather of words, and those words serve as specific incantations that invite us into and guide us through the universe of the imagination. Language is the apparatus—the magic dust—by which a writer performs his miracles. . . . Beyond anything, I think, a writer is someone entranced by the power of language to create a magic show of the imagination, to make the dead sit up and talk, to shine light into the darkness of the great human mysteries . . . (177)

This vision of the writer again suggests his earlier claim that in Vietnam the United States was fighting forces that twentieth century science could not understand, and that he is committed to exploring the nature of those forces as fully as he can. But even more so it suggests again his vision of the shaman who by telling stories summons "a collective dream"; here, too, O'Brien links storytelling to religion, citing not only the shaman but also Christ as a storyteller and miracle worker in one (177). Writing is, he claims, essentially an act of faith, a way of exploring "that which cannot be known by empirical means" and moving toward "epiphany or understanding or enlightenment" (179).

This vision of the role of the writer is perhaps what most fully elevates O'Brien from mere "war writer" to speaker to and for the whole of humanity. And this language, in both "The Magic Show" and in "The Lives of the

Dead," seems allusive again in that it is almost Joycean. The narrator persona here closes in an act of grand affirmation of the powers of the writer to transform lives, to raise the dead, sounding "like a Vietnam version of Joyce's Stephen Dedalus" (Myers 154). Certainly throughout the story—when he speaks of the writer for whom "memory and imagination and language combine to make spirits in the head"—he echoes young Stephen's vision of himself in *A Portrait of the Artist as a Young Man* as a "priest of the eternal imagination, transmuting the daily bread of experience into the radiant body of ever-living life."

Finally, then, "The Lives of the Dead" ties together all of the focal elements—setting, protagonists both collective and emerging, storytelling, allusiveness—which O'Brien has been working with all along to bind *The Things They Carried* together as composite novel. The richness and complexity of this book—and the composite novel form—make it difficult to determine where one focal element ends and another begins, where one can examine setting without examining character, or examine an "emerging protagonist" without examining storytelling, and so on. But O'Brien is pleased to have it so, it seems; as many of his statements indicate, he rejects the rigorously analytical vision of the real for one that allows more room for mystery and relatedness. In writing *The Things They Carried*, he has posited his own vision of the real, not just of his experience in Vietnam but of perennial facets of experience that belong to the whole of humanity.

Works Cited

Beidler, Philip. *Re-Writing America: Vietnam Authors in Their Generation*. Athens: University of Georgia Press, 1991.

Dunn, Maggie, and Morris, Ann. *The Composite Novel: The Short Story Cycle in Transition*. New York: Twayne, 1995.

Kaplan, Steven. *Understanding Tim O'Brien*. Columbia: University of South Carolina Press, 1995.

Myers, Thomas. "Tim O'Brien." *Dictionary of Literary Biography*. Vol. 152, *American Novelists Since World War II*, fourth series. Ed. James R. Giles and Wanda H. Giles. Detroit: Bruccoli Clark Layman, 1995.

O'Brien, Tim. Interview. *Anything Can Happen: Interviews with Contemporary American Novelists*. Ed. Tom LeClair and Larry McCaffery. Urbana: University of Illinois Press, 1983.

———. "An Interview with Tim O'Brien." By Steven Kaplan. *Missouri Review* 14: 1991: 94–108.

———. "The Magic Show." *Writers on Writing*. Ed. Robert Pack and Jay Parini. Hanover: Middlebury College Press, 1991.

———. *The Things They Carried*. New York: Penguin, 1990.

MATS TEGMARK

The Perspectives of Other Characters

"What you have to do [. . .] is trust your own story. Get the hell out of
the way and let it tell itself." (116)

—Mitchell Sanders

One of the main differences in communicative approach between
Things and the other two narratives [*If I Die in a Combat Zone* and *Going
after Cacciato*] is the relative importance of, and large space attributed to,
the perspectives of characters other than "Tim O'Brien" as protagonist.
Not only are these characters more developed, they also have two new
functions in this text—that of protagonist and that of what I call secondary narrator: in two of the stories, "The Things They Carried" and
"Speaking of Courage," a character other than "O'Brien" functions as
focalizer, constituting the main perspective from which the reader per-
ceives the story; in three stories another character functions as a kind of
secondary narrator; that is, the reader is presented with a story within the
story—what Genette calls a "metadiegetic narrative" (228)—told by one
of the other characters. Besides these two new communicative functions
performed by other characters, there are also a number of very short stories in which more marginal characters are focused on only externally, in a
more conventional fashion. The fact that *Things* features other characters
both as protagonists and secondary narrators is also in accordance with

17

its generic form. Unlike the unity of form found in *If I Die* and *Cacciato*, the relative independence of the stories in *Things* makes it possible for the implied author to attribute these additional, or extended, functions to other characters. In the discussion below I will first look at the two stories featuring another protagonist, then at six short stories providing the reader with an external perspective on some of the other characters, and lastly turn to the three stories where other characters function as secondary narrators. As before, the main emphasis of my analyses below will be on the specific roles that these three different uses of other characters create for the reader. As we will see, the reader is expected to perform such different tasks as identifying with, listening to, and laughing at these other characters.

Other Protagonists: "The Things They Carried"

The first story featuring a protagonist other than "O'Brien" is the opening title story, "The Things They Carried." Like most stories in this volume, it is divided into two parallel narrative lines, each dominated by a specific narrative perspective. The first perspective presented is that of the main character, or protagonist, of the story, the platoon leader Lieutenant Jimmy Cross. The story told about this protagonist is in short the following: Cross keeps thinking about a girl called Martha, from whom he receives letters he wishes were love letters; time and again he disappears into his daydreams as he leads his men through the perils of the war. When a soldier called Ted Lavender is killed by a sniper, Cross takes all the blame on himself for neglecting his duties as a leader. As a consequence, he burns Martha's letters and vows to himself never again to let his daydreams interfere with his responsibilities as leader.

Parallel to this story a more descriptive, non-narrative account is given, in which the narrator enumerates the many physical and mental "things" the average foot soldier carried along as he walked through the jungles of Vietnam. So whereas in the sections about Jimmy Cross the narrator tells a *specific* story—with specific events, characters, and settings—in the other parts he lets the reader know about all the things the grunts *generally* carried with them. In other words, whereas the first line is dominated by the perspective of Jimmy Cross, the second can be said to be dominated by the perspective of the average grunt, presented to the reader through a very overt and seemingly omniscient narrator who appears to have firsthand knowledge about the subject.

What is it then that these two perspectives communicate in the story? What are their features and functions, and how are they presented to the reader?

Jimmy Cross as Dreamer

The main aspect of the war experience communicated through the perspective of Jimmy Cross in this story is one we recognize both from other stories in the volume and from other O'Brien narratives—especially *Cacciato*—namely, the habit soldiers have of dreaming themselves away from the immediate reality of the war. What makes this story different from the others dealing with this phenomenon, however, is that the protagonist dreaming here is not the protagonist of the whole volume. As the reader finds out when s/he comes to the next story, Jimmy Cross is only one out of many other characters featured in the volume. Moreover, unlike the "O'Briens" the reader meets in *If I Die* and in the other stories of *Things*, and unlike Paul Berlin, Jimmy Cross is not a private, but a commanding officer and platoon leader. These differences might not seem so important at first, but they do help to prevent the reader from getting the impression that daydreaming of this kind is something only experienced by protagonists clearly modeled on the author, or that it is something exclusive for the private, usually drafted, soldier. Besides, the fact that Jimmy Cross is a platoon leader makes his lack of concentration seem even more consequential as he is responsible for more lives than his own. Reminding "himself that his obligation was not to be loved but to lead" (25), he "would accept the blame for what had happened to Ted Lavender" (24).

The way this dangerous mental escape is communicated is by making Jimmy Cross the main focalizer of the story.[13] Right from the beginning the reader is presented with an inside view of what goes on in his head. Most of the time, the workings of his mind are explained by the narrator, who has more or less complete access to his mind: looking at a picture Martha sent him, for example, "Lieutenant Cross wondered who had taken the picture, because he knew she had boyfriends, because he loved her so much, and because he could see the shadow of the picture-taker spreading out against the brick wall" (5). Here we see how most of what is said about Cross is filtered through the explaining perspective of the narrator, and thus the implied author can be said to orchestrate two perspectives at the same time. The anaphoric use of the word *because* indicates the narrator's presence, and his intention to make everything clear. But there are a few instances where the reader is provided with a more direct rendition of Cross's thoughts: "He wanted to know her. Intimate secrets: Why poetry? Why so sad? Why that grayness in her eyes? Why so alone? Not lonely, just alone—riding her bike across campus or sitting off by herself in the cafeteria—even dancing, she danced alone—and it was the aloneness that filled him with love" (12). In this way, then, the reader gets to follow Jimmy

Cross in his escapes from the war, and s/he gets to understand that these daydreams are hard to wake up from; even though he burns Martha's letters and photos after Lavender's death, he realizes himself that "[y]ou couldn't burn the blame" (22). As the all-explaining narrator makes clear, "the letters were in his head. Even now, without photographs, Lieutenant Cross could see Martha playing volleyball in her white gym shorts and yellow T-shirt. He could see her moving in the rain" (23). In short, one can say that in these sections of the story the implied author makes the narrator tell the reader about, and explain, the experience of daydreams, rather than as in *Cacciato* have the reader experience the daydreaming directly through the extensive use of interior monologue and visualization. Thus the reader's role here is more passive as there are only small and few gaps for him or her to fill, at least when it comes to constructing the protagonist's character.

Another common experience among the soldiers in Vietnam also communicated through the perspective of Jimmy Cross is that of being completely cut off from the rest of the world. In spite of the fact that the soldiers, as in this story, literally carried all the things of their western world along with them, life in Vietnam was often experienced as so different from that at home that the United States was referred to as simply the "World." This difference is foregrounded in a number of places in the story. Toward the end Jimmy Cross comes to the conclusion that his dreams of him and Martha together on the Jersey shore, "carrying nothing" (10), were nothing but pure "fantasies": "He was a soldier, after all" (23); and she was a junior and English major at Mount Sebastian. "Henceforth, when he thought about Martha, it would be only to think that she belonged elsewhere. He would shut down the daydreams. This was not Mount Sebastian, it was another world, where there were no pretty poems or midterm exams, a place where men died because of carelessness and gross stupidity" (23–24). The idea that the soldiers in Vietnam live in a completely different world from that experienced at home, a world governed by its own laws of nature, is taken up again in "Sweetheart," which will be discussed below.

THE LOAD OF THE GRUNTS

While the sections about Jimmy Cross tell the story of what this protagonist carried along in his mind at a specific time, and what his carrying-on eventually led to, the other sections of the story are made up of the narrator's expository discourse on what the other grunts in the platoon generally carried. Hence, the focus in these sections is less concentrated, and the experience communicated less determined. Instead of following up on one specific load, like the daydreams of Jimmy Cross, the narrator enumerates over a hundred things, physical as well as psychological, carried by the average foot soldier. What kind of experience all these things carried add up to is never stated, however; instead it is up to the reader to put all these data together and construct for him- or herself an idea of what it must have been like to "walk" under this enormous load.

Thus, the basic narrative strategy employed by the implied author when it comes to communicating the experience of the grunt in these sections is to have the narrator present the reader with facts and figures—down to the most minute detail and exact weight—of what the grunts carried. Nor is the order arbitrary in which these things are enumerated. As the narrator makes clear from the beginning: "The things carried were largely determined by necessity," and what turns out to be highest on the grunt's list of necessities is not particularly motivated by military concerns. Contrary to what might have been expected, guns and ammunition are not found on this initial list: "[a]mong the necessities or near-necessities were P-38 can openers, pocket knives, heat tabs, wristwatches, dog tags, mosquito repellent, chewing gum, candy, cigarettes, salt tablets, packets of Kool-Aid, lighters, matches, sewing kits, Military Payment Certificates, C-rations, and two or three canteens of water" (4). Military gear such as helmets and flak jackets seem to be carried just as much because it was "SOP" (Standard Operating Procedure) as because they were necessities. More important than this heavy equipment seem to be the many items peculiar to the individual:

> Ted Lavender carried six or seven ounces of premium dope, which for him was a necessity. Mitchell Sanders, the RTO, carried condoms. Norman Bowker carried a diary. Rat Kiley carried comic books. Kiowa, a devout Baptist, carried an illustrated New Testament that had been presented to him by his father, who taught Sunday school in Oklahoma City, Oklahoma. As a hedge against bad times, however, Kiowa also carried his grandmother's distrust of the white man, his grandfather's old hunting hatchet. Necessity dictated. (4–5)

What this initial list of necessities above all suggests to the reader is the very basic *human* side of the grunt's life. What they need to survive turns out to be what we all need to survive in our daily life: food, clothing, and protection. The last lines quoted also show that another function of these sections is to introduce these grunts as individuals whose baggage is determined by their personality; and in turn, the reader constructs their personality from the things they carry. In other words, we are what we carry. From this initial list, then, we can say that, in brief, grunt life is first of all human life, with both its basics and peculiarities; only secondly, or sometimes thirdly, is it characterized as military life.

As hinted at above, what characterizes the way in which the catalogues of things carried are presented is the explaining, detailed, and systematic, or as Kaplan puts it, "academic," style of the narrator (*Understanding* 172). Just as in his descriptions of Jimmy Cross's mental escapes, the narrator is here fond of the explanatory word *because*. But as Kaplan has pointed out, the sentences initiated by this word do not explain all that much. I would say that the main effect of the word here is ironic, as in: "Because you could die so quickly, each man carried at least one large compress bandage, usually in the helmet band for easy access. Because the nights were cold, and because the monsoons were wet, each carried a green plastic poncho that could be used as a raincoat or groundsheet or makeshift tent." In other words, humor is produced by the obvious inefficacy or hopeless inadequacy of the remedy in relation to the problem—a plastic poncho is about as useful in a monsoon as a compress is against sudden death. The same academic and ironic tone is apparent in the narrator's description of the grunts' language: "To carry something was to hump it, as when Lieutenant Jimmy Cross humped his love for Martha up the hills and through the swamps. In its intransitive form, to hump meant to walk, or to march, but it implied burdens far beyond the intransitive" (5).

The last quotation above betrays the narrator's predilection for witty juxtapositions. Usually these juxtapositions consist of unexpected combinations of physical and mental burdens carried by the grunts, as in the following two sentences: "He [Cross] carried a strobe light and the responsibility for the lives of his men" (6); and: "Depending on numerous factors, such as topography and psychology, the riflemen carried anything from 12 to 20 magazines" (7). In short one can say that the emotional engagement characteristic of the narrator's discourse in the more "autobiographical" stories—dominated by the narrator as character—is replaced by the more detached and factual style of this academic voice. Nowhere is this detachment more conspicuous than in the many objective, almost deterministic, references to Ted Lavender's death, containing traces of black humor: "Ted Lavender, who was scared, carried tranquilizers until he was shot in the head outside the village of Than Khe in mid-April" (4). No fewer than seven times is Lavender's death mentioned in passing like this—each time in an adverbial subclause. These impersonal, almost disrespectful, references to Lavender's fate can be said to foreshadow the many subsequent examples of how death was derided in the soldiers' use of language.

What consequences, then, does all this detailed, detached explaining by the narrator have for the actual act of reading? At first it would seem that the reader's role is one of mere passive perception of the narrator's ready-made explanations. However, what is being communicated here are not the *things* carried, but the *experience of carrying* these things. This means that what is explained in such detail by the narrator is only the texture of the soldiers' baggage, the raw material as it were; the construction of the actual experience has to be completed by the reader. Only by linking these details together can the reader get an idea of what it meant to carry this collective burden. The final product, in other words, is more than the sum of the parts. Thus the communicatory structure of this story mirrors that of the whole volume.

Although the experience communicated here has to be constructed to a large extent by the reader from "objective" catalogues of details of this type, there are a few instances, especially toward the end of the story, where the narrator diverts from his academic style and reverts to a more involved, emotional, and informal kind of narration. It is as if the lists of things carried are not enough, as if the narrator feels compelled to point a few things out with a little more zest in order to make sure that his narratee—and in turn the reader—really can picture what it was like to carry these "things." The first time this type of stylistic digression occurs is when the narrator enumerates the equipment, mostly explosives, carried along on search-and-destroy missions. In the middle of his catalogue the narrator starts describing how the searching and blowing of tunnels usually was carried out: "whoever drew the number 17 would strip off his gear and crawl in headfirst with a flashlight and Lieutenant Cross's .45 caliber pistol. The rest of them would fan out as security" (11). In the middle of this description—in mid-sentence, actually—the narrator switches pronouns, from the detached *they* to the much more involved and informal *you*, and the viewpoint moves from the narrator's external perspective to that of the soldiers sitting by the hole, imagining themselves going down. As a consequence, the register changes from formal academic to informal grunt language:

> They would sit down or kneel, not facing the hole, listening to the ground beneath them, imagining cobwebs and ghosts, whatever was down there—the tunnel walls squeezing in—how the flashlight seemed impossibly heavy in the hand and how it was tunnel vision in the very strictest sense, compression in all ways, even time, and how you had to wiggle in—ass and elbows—a swallowed-up feeling—and how you found yourself worrying about odd things: Will your flashlight go dead? Do rats carry rabies? If you screamed, how far would the sound carry? Would your buddies hear it? Would they have the courage to drag you out? In some respects, though not many, the waiting was worse than the tunnel itself. Imagination was a killer. (11)

In the second part of this passage we see how the narrator literally takes the perspective of the grunt, imagining himself going down a tunnel, voicing his actual thoughts, thereby inviting his narratee to join him. Not until the final sentence of the paragraph does the viewpoint return to the narrator's more detached and explicatory perspective.

Toward the end of the story, the lists of things carried become less material, with burdens more psychological and mental than physical. Although stylistically and grammatically the narrator remains detached most of the time, the perspective of the grunt is still strongly evoked as the narrator's descriptions now are more directly focused on the mental experience as such. This means that whereas in the early parts of the story the reader had to start more or less from scratch in his or her construction of the actual experience, here s/he is guided more directly by the narrator. Many of these direct descriptions of the grunt experience we recognize from the earlier narratives; the following passage, which starts with a description of how the grunts carried the land itself with them, echoes—at times word by word—much of what is said in "Days" in *If I Die* and "The Way It Mostly Was" in *Cacciato*:

> The whole atmosphere, they carried it, the humidity, the monsoons, the stink of fungus and decay, all of it, they carried gravity. They moved like mules. By daylight they took sniper fire, at night they were mortared, but it was not battle, it was just the endless march, village to village, without purpose, nothing won or lost. They marched for the sake of the march. They plodded along slowly, dumbly, leaning forward against the heat, unthinking, all blood and bone, simple grunts, soldiering with their legs, toiling up the hills and down into the paddies and across the rivers and up again and down, just humping, one step and then the next and then another, but no volition, no will, because it was automatic, it was anatomy, and the war was entirely a matter of posture and carriage, the hump was everything, a kind of inertia, a kind of emptiness, a dullness of desire and intellect and conscience and hope and human sensibility. Their principles were in their feet. (15)

The second to last sentence above is a good example of how the narrator's discourse, through its seemingly unending clauses, typically suggests the experience of an endless march.

Another recurrent aspect of the grunt experience which is brought up toward the end of the story is the problem of how to carry *oneself*, especially in times of constant fear and immediate danger. Although

> [f]or the most part they carried themselves with poise, a kind of dignity, [...] there were times of panic, when they squealed

or wanted to squeal but couldn't, when they twitched and made moaning sounds and covered their heads and said Dear Jesus and flopped around on the earth and fired their weapons blindly and cringed and sobbed and begged for the noise to stop and went wild and made stupid promises to themselves and to God and to their mothers and fathers, hoping not to die. (18–19)

This experience, too, we recognize from both the previous books, but, as in the example above, the difference is that here the experience is explained, in so many words, whereas in the previous, much longer narratives, the reader has time to experience the dullness of the march, or the panic of the ambush, in a more direct way through the process and experience of reading. The following sentence, for example, is a perfect description of what is dramatized in *If I Die* and *Cacciato*, as well as in a number of stories in this volume, for that matter: "Some carried themselves with a sort of wistful resignation, others with pride or stiff soldierly discipline or good humor or macho zeal. They were afraid of dying but they were even more afraid to show it" (19).

However, when the narrator describes how "they used a hard vocabulary to contain the terrible softness" inside them, and how "they were actors" using "grunt lingo" in their attempt "to encyst and destroy the reality of death itself" (20), it is as if the implied author realizes that here the reader is in need of a dramatized example. Consequently, s/he is provided with a short dialogue where Mitchell Sanders and Henry Dobbins joke about the recently killed Ted Lavender.

The final aspect of the grunt experience taken up in the narrator's lists of things carried—how they were "carried away" in their daydreams—is also exemplified right after it has been introduced. This time the reader is presented with passages which can best be described as a mixture of stream-of-consciousness and interior monologue, where the reader's viewpoint enters the perspective of the dreaming grunt as he imagines himself aboard the freedom bird:

> but it was more than a plane, it was a real bird, a big sleek silver bird with feathers and talons and high screeching. They were flying. The weights fell off; there was nothing to bear. They laughed and held on tight, feeling the cold slap of wind and altitude, soaring, thinking *It's over, I'm gone!* [. . .] *Sin loi!* they yelled. *I'm sorry, motherfuckers, but I'm out of it, I'm goofed, I'm on a space cruise, I'm gone!* (22)

This final aspect of the grunt experience—how the soldiers let themselves be "carried away" to the "World" in their dreams—is also paralleled in the more specific story about Jimmy Cross. Hence, the two narrative lines can be said to meet at the end. This means that in the act of reading the story the reader has two kinds of gaps or blanks to fill in: s/he has to construct the general experience of the grunt by linking all the things carried together; simultaneously, s/he has to relate this collective experience to the more specific one of the protagonist Jimmy Cross.

To conclude, in the analysis above we have seen how the opening title story, "The Things They Carried," deals with a number of experiences central also in O'Brien's two earlier Vietnam narratives, such as dreaming oneself away to another world, the problem of carrying oneself with poise in times of fear and terror, and the experience of being a toiling mule "humping" without thoughts and meaning, on a march without end or purpose. The difference, however, is that here all these "things" are "carried" in one and the same short story. Still, in spite of the brevity of the text, the story does manage to intertwine the expository and condensed discourse of the narrator with a more involved type of narration—what I have called stylistic digressions—in which the reader is engaged in a more active way; that is, the academic presentation of facts and details is supplemented with exemplification and focalization through both the perspective of the general grunt and that of the protagonist Jimmy Cross. The employment of these different narrative strategies and styles in one and the same story makes "The Things They Carried" a relatively short but highly representative example of O'Brien's communicatory style.[14]

Other Protagonists: "Speaking of Courage"

The other long story in this volume featuring a protagonist other than the young "O'Brien" is the one entitled "Speaking of Courage." The aspect of the war experience dealt with here is in short the typical post-war problem of having no one to talk to about one's haunting war memories, the experience of coming home to a dead town where no one is interested in the kind of stories a Vietnam veteran has to tell. The way this classical experience is communicated is by making the troubled mind of Norman Bowker, the protagonist, the focal point of the story. In fact, as the narrator in this story functions merely as an anonymous storytelling voice—constituting no real ideological narrative perspective of its own—the only perspective for the reader to take is that of Bowker as he drives his father's car around and around the town lake. The fact that the reader's viewpoint is situated inside the car, and inside Bowker's mind, is clear already in the opening sentences: "The war was over and there was no place in particular to go. Norman Bowker followed the tar road on its seven-mile loop around the lake, then he started all over again, driving slowly, feeling safe *inside* his father's big Chevy, now and then *looking out* on the lake to watch the boats and waterskiers and scenery" (157, emphasis added). Throughout the story then, the reader gets to follow what goes on in Bowker's mind during the four, five hours that the story spans—in much the same way as the reader of *Cacciato* gets to monitor Berlin's mind at the observation post.

The only subperspective with which the reader is presented is that of Bowker himself back in Vietnam, because the central memory around which his mind is circling, in the same way that his car is circling the lake, is that of how he failed to rescue his friend Kiowa from drowning in a field of human excrement. Thus, Bowker can be said to be "divided into two halves," one physical and one mental; like the lake, "[o]ne half still glistened, the other was caught in shadow" (169). This division means that the gap the reader has to fill in this story is that of how his terrible experience in Vietnam has turned Bowker into the alienated, apathetic person he is in the story's present. With the guidance of this subperspective, or substory, s/he will try to find out why he so desperately needs someone with whom to "speak of courage."

Before I go into a more detailed analysis of how Bowker's experience is made present to the reader, a few words need to be said about the different versions of this story. When "Speaking of Courage" was first published in 1976, it was published as an "orphan" story, initially envisioned as a chapter in *Cacciato*. But, as O'Brien himself says in a 1980 preface to a separate publication of the story, "*Going After Cacciato* was a war story; 'Speaking of Courage' was a post-war story."[15] As it appears in *Things*, the names have been changed, naturally, but more substantial changes have also been made; actually, almost half of the story has been rewritten for the new version. The main difference when it comes to the role of the reader is that in the new version the central memory around which the story is revolving is given much more space; about four pages have been added in which Bowker imagines himself telling his father about the night he "could've won the Silver Star for valor" (165). This means that, whereas in the original story the reader had just one perspective with which to identify, that of Paul Berlin driving around the town lake, the reader of the new version, as mentioned, is presented also with a strong subperspective of the protagonist in Vietnam; thus s/he is in a better position to understand the protagonist's agony of having no one with whom to share his memory.

In Search of a Listener

What makes this story interesting in the context of a study of the communication between implied author and reader is that—not unlike many other stories in this volume—it thematizes communication itself, or rather, the lack of communication characteristic of Bowker's postwar experience. To begin with, the title is ambiguous, because Bowker never *speaks* of courage;

he *thinks* about speaking of it. Moreover, he never speaks of courage, rather, what troubles him is his *lack* of courage, the fact that he never did perform that courageous act of saving Kiowa from drowning. Therefore, the only level on which the title can be said to ring true—that is, where communication does take place—is that on which the implied author communicates with his reader. In other words, when no one else is listening to Bowker's story of how he failed to win the Silver Star, the reader is.

The alienation and lack of communication that characterize Bowker's relation to his family and hometown are expressed in a number of different ways, both directly and indirectly. In addition to pointing to Bowker's desire to talk about his war memories by means of a number of imaginary conversations that he carries on in his mind—especially with his father and his high-school sweetheart Sally Gustafson, nee Kramer—the implied author of the new version has added a number of direct statements indicating this wish: "If Sally had not been married, or if his father were not such a baseball fan, it would have been a good time to talk" (160). What is referred to here is the tragic irony of the fact that this day, when no one wants to hear him talk of his and his friends' sacrifices for their country, happens to be the Fourth of July. But even if he were to stop and talk to Sally, he realizes that "he would not say a word about how he'd almost won the Silver Star for valor" (160). Thus he never stops to talk to her; instead, "feeling safe inside his father's big Chevy" (157), he keeps driving, hiding from the townspeople, "taking pleasure in the steady sounds of the engine and air conditioning" (162). This alienation from his own hometown, which he considers deaf and dumb to his concerns, is further underlined in the new version, in which Bowker compares himself to a tourist:

> A tour bus feeling, in a way, except the town he was touring seemed dead. Through the windows, as if in a stop-motion photograph, the place looked as if it had been hit by nerve gas, everything still and lifeless, even the people. The town could not talk, and would not listen. "How'd you like to hear about the war?" he might have asked, but the place could only blink and shrug. It had no memory, therefore no guilt. [. . .] It was a brisk, polite town. It did not know shit about shit, and did not care to know. (162–63)

The feeling of alienation and lack of communication that Bowker experiences in his relation to his "lifeless" hometown is further evoked and intensified by what little and awkward contact he does have with the outer world in this story, because this contact is anything but human. In the seclusion of his "safe" car he listens to the tired voice of the radio announcer, a "voice rocking

itself into a deep Sunday snooze" (166). The only function this one-way communication has is to confirm the lethargy of the whole setting—the high
temperature and the passing of time. Apart from the obnoxious young carhop
at the A&W, Bowker's only contact with the world outside the Chevy is in
the form of an impersonal voice; his hamburger orders are only taken through
"an intercom attached to a steel post" (170). The "conversation" Bowker carries
on with this "tinny voice" (171) is charged with more tragic irony: the reader,
by now familiar with Bowker's haunted memory and his desperate need to
talk about the war—especially about how the incoming mortars made mud
craters in which Kiowa died—witnesses how, when he finally talks to someone, that someone mimics the language of war, and especially that of an artil-
lery soldier:

> The intercom squeaked and said, "Order."
> "Mama Burger and fries," Norman Bowker said.
> "Affirmative, copy clear. No rootie-tootie?"
> "Rootie-tootie?"
> "You know, man—root beer."
> "A small one."
> "Roger-dodger. Repeat: one Mama, one fries, one small beer.
> Fire for effect. Stand by."
> The intercom squeaked and went dead.
> "Out," said Norman Bowker. (170)

In other words, the town knows how to talk *like* a soldier, but not how to
talk *to* him about his experience.

BOWKER'S STORY

When all attempts at communication with his hometown fail, Bowker
imagines an addressee, and the only one he can imagine more or less willing to listen to his tales is his father. Prodded by the imagined exhortation
of his father—"So tell me" (161)—Bowker begins to tell the story of how he
"almost won the Silver Star for valor" (160). Initially, he tells it by actually
formulating the very sentences he would use, given as actual quotations in
the text. Starting with a description of the river Song Tra Bong, and how it
flooded during the rainy season, Bowker soon interrupts himself, asking his
imagined interlocutor: "You really want to hear this?" (162). Even though
he makes his father tell him to go on, it takes Bowker another loop around
the lake—and the reader another two pages—before he is ready to pick up
the thread again, this time remembering the night they bivouacked in a
filthy field by the river, a field which turns out to be the "village toilet"—a

"goddamn *shit* field" (164). The field itself Bowker manages to describe, still in his own words, before he has to interrupt himself again, making another loop in the Chevy, and making the reader wait for another page, increasing the tension further. When he returns to his haunting story for the third time, however, to tell what happened in that field during that night, it is as if the memory becomes too difficult to actually formulate in his own words—even though it is "only" in his imagination. Thus this final part of Bowker's story is never "spoken" by himself, instead it is presented indirectly from his perspective, but not only from his perspective in the car circling the lake, but also from his subperspective experiencing the remembered event itself. The viewpoint, in other words, moves all the way back to Vietnam. Consequently, in the final description of Kiowa's drowning and Bowker's futile attempt to rescue him, the reader is there with him:

> he grabbed Kiowa by the boot and tried to pull him out. He pulled hard but Kiowa was gone, and then suddenly he felt himself going too. He could taste it. The shit was in his nose and eyes. There were flares and mortar rounds, and the stink was everywhere—it was inside him, in his lungs—and he could no longer tolerate it. Not here, he thought. Not like this. He released Kiowa's boot and watched it slide away. Slowly, working his way up, he hoisted himself out of the deep mud, and then he lay still and tasted the shit in his mouth and closed his eyes and listened to the rain and explosions and bubbling sounds.
> He was alone. (168)

Only when this scene is over—and when the reader's viewpoint has moved back into the safety of the Chevy—can Bowker imagine himself talking about it again: "'I didn't flip out,' he would've said. 'I was cool. If things had gone right, if it hadn't been for that smell, I could've won the Silver Star'" (168–69).

In conclusion, then, we can say that in this story the reader first of all takes the perspective of Norman Bowker as he drives around the town lake wishing he had someone to talk to, someone who would really listen. But parallel to this s/he also gets to accompany Bowker back to Vietnam, and there, from his subperspective, s/he gets to witness the event which he so desperately wants to talk about. Thus, knowing what it is that is haunting Bowker's memory, the reader can better understand his need for a listener; and conversely, knowing how desperate Bowker is to talk about this haunted memory, the reader can better (re)construct for him- or herself the emotional impact of Bowker's actual experience in the field itself. In this way then, the two perspectives of the story can be said to dialogically influence each other. To further guide the reader in correlating these two perspectives and to make him or her see the enormous difference between the reality in Bowker's prairie town and that of Vietnam, the implied author has provided him or her with a number of symbolic parallels: the lake—the field, the fireworks—the mortar and flares, as well as the mocking of military language. In the end, these two perspectives can be said to meet: having circled the lake twelve times—suggesting a tour of duty—Bowker stops the car and walks into the filthy water; that is, having mentally circled his memory of the field a number of times, he finally confronts it by having it visualized in his imagination. As we have seen, this narrative strategy means that in the end, it is the reader who functions as the exclusive witness; when all of Bowker's surroundings seem dead, and unwilling, or even unable, to listen to his story, the reader, as an active participant in the text, will fill the gap where the listener should be.

Other Characters; or, The Things Their Minds Made Them Do

Scattered throughout the volume are six very short stories, each about two or three pages long and centered on one or two of the minor characters.[16] Although these very often comic characters are at the center of the stories, they cannot be called protagonists in a strict sense. Actually, three of the four characters figuring in these stories can be characterized as *antagonists*. They are not presented as particularly agreeable characters, and, unlike the stories discussed above where the implied author asks the reader to identify with the characters, s/he is here invited to laugh at them. The only one of these characters that is presented with some sympathy is Henry Dobbins; that he is one of the more likeable characters is evident also from the fact that he is among the group of characters to whom the whole narrative is dedicated.

What these stories have in common—both with each other and with the rest of the volume—is that they deal with what goes on in the heads of these soldiers. Thus, like the stories discussed above, these short anecdotes are centered around what the mental *experience* of war makes soldiers do. As before, then, it is the mind—and especially the imagination—of the soldier that the implied author is trying to say something about. The main difference, however, is the *way* in which these short stories can be said to communicate the mental makeup of the soldiers. Whereas the longer stories, most of which have been discussed above, provide the reader with more or less direct access to the mind of the protagonist through the extensive use of focalization, these anecdotes offer the reader nothing but an outside perspective, usually that of the narrator remembering and/or the young "O'Brien" observing the character in question. Typically, the way in which a specific mental experience, often an emotion or a state of mind, is suggested in these short stories is by first presenting the reader with a more or less subjective characterization of the character and then having him—it is always a he—illustrate this typical character trait through some kind of final act, physical or verbal. In short, a fitting subtitle for these six stories would be "The Things Their Minds Made Them Do," to continue the author's phraseology. What the reader has to do, then, is to see how the initial characterization is related to the final act: is that act a confirmation or a contradiction of previous characterization, or does it point to some other character trait or experience?

Let us see how this pattern functions in practice. In the story entitled "Stockings" the reader is first presented with a direct description of a character:

> Henry Dobbins was a good man, and a superb soldier, but sophis-
> tication was not his strong suit. The ironies went beyond him. In
> many ways he was like America itself, big and strong, full of good
> intentions, a roll of fat jiggling at his belly, slow of foot but always
> plodding along, always when you needed him, a believer in
> the virtues of simplicity and directness and hard labor. Like his
> country, too, Dobbins was drawn toward sentimentality. (129)

That this very subjective characterization emanates from the perspective of the narrator is also evident in what follows: "Even now, twenty years later, I can see him wrapping his girlfriend's pantyhose around his neck before heading out on ambush" (129). In this way the reader learns of Dobbins's "one eccentricity"; his girlfriend's nylons "were a talisman for him. They kept him safe." The narrator even names the character trait alluded to: "Like many of us in Vietnam, Dobbins felt the pull of superstition, and he believed firmly and absolutely in the protective power of the stockings" (129–30). At the end of the story, however, the reader finds out that his girlfriend has dumped him, and s/he is presented with the following final scene: "It was a hard blow. Dobbins went quiet for a while, staring down at her letter, then after a time he took out the stockings and tied them around his neck as a comforter. / 'No sweat,' he said. 'The magic doesn't go away'" (130). Thus, even though Dobbins has already been characterized as superstitious, it is only after this final act that the reader can get an understanding of how strong this "pull of superstition" actually can become in times of war; and when he trips a mine that turns out to be a dud, he turns the whole platoon into believers in his stockings.

But it is not always the case that the final act can be said to confirm or enhance the characterization preceding it. In "Church," the next story in the volume, Dobbins is further characterized—this time more indirectly by his speech—as the typical American, wishing to be good: 'Just being *nice* to people, that's all. Being decent,'" he tells Kiowa. When the platoon sets up its base in an abandoned pagoda tended by two monks, Dobbins's likeable character seems to be confirmed once again as the two monks "[take] a special liking for Henry Dobbins" (134); they even help him disassemble and clean his machine gun. At the end, however, when the two monks have finished cleaning the gun, Dobbins "[hands] each of them a can of peaches and a chocolate bar" and tells them to "beat it," then telling Kiowa: "All you can do is be nice. Treat them decent, you know" (136). Thus, from Dobbins's final line, the reader is likely to come to the conclusion that Dobbins's good intentions are nothing *but* good intentions. "Doing good" for Dobbins is tantamount to handing out C-rations; the fact that he and his platoon have turned the monks' pagoda "into a little fortress" (133) does not seem to contradict this goodness. The parallel to the whole U.S. presence in Vietnam is conspicuous.

Although Dobbins's good intentions are not always so sophisticatedly implemented, at least he tries to "be nice." This, however, is more than can be said about some of the other characters figuring in these short anecdotal stories. The character showing the least amount of understanding of, and respect for, the Vietnamese people is Azar in the story called "Style." What Azar— and the rest of the platoon for that matter—cannot understand is why, after her whole family has been killed, a young girl keeps dancing in the dirt by the place where her house used to be. What makes Azar's behavior particularly unsympathetic, however, is not the fact that he keeps commenting on the girl's dancing, but that he cannot accept his lack of understanding for what it is; at the end the reader learns that later the same day, when "Azar mocked the girl's dancing," Dobbins "lifted him up high and carried him over to a deep well and asked if he wanted to be dumped in. Azar said no. 'All right, then,' Henry Dobbins said, 'dance right.'" What seems to be implied here is that even though you cannot understand the behavior of another people, you should show some respect; in other words, there is a limit to what kind of "style" you can have, especially for Dobbins who, in spite of his clumsy movements, tries to adopt a "nice" style: Dobbins, the reader learns, "moved gracefully for such a big man" (154).

The most comic of these characters who behave awkwardly due to the tension in their minds is perhaps Curt Lemon in "The Dentist." In the initial description of this character, the narrator makes no secret of the fact that he does not find Lemon's character traits "impressive": "He had an opinion of himself, I think, that was too high for his own good. Or maybe it was the reverse. Maybe it was a low opinion that he kept trying to erase." To make it clear to the reader how important one's opinion of oneself can be—and what it can make a character like Lemon do—the implied author has the narrator "tell a quick Curt Lemon story": in spite of his "tough soldier role" (95)—professedly he enjoyed combat—"there was something about a dentist that just gave him the creeps." Going into the dentist's tent one day, "[h]e fainted even before the man touched him" (96). As the narrator explains, "[a]nyone else would've laughed it off, but for Curt Lemon it was too much. The embarrassment must've turned a screw in his head." At night he wakes up the dentist and makes him "[yank] out a perfectly good tooth. There was some pain, no doubt, but in the morning Curt Lemon was all smiles" (97).

Thus, once again it is illustrated to the reader that in war—as in everyday life—people are much more willing to accept physical rather than mental suffering. Also illustrated in this story as well as in the other stories is the fact that foot soldiers—like people in general—are social beings. They think very much about who they are and why they do the things they do, and most importantly, they care more about what other people think than about their own—and others'—physical well being. In the final analysis, this is also why many young men go to war—they are too "embarrassed not to" (62). Therefore, in spite of their eccentricities, I believe that what is primarily communicated in these short stories is very much the *human* side of these grunts. In spite of Dobbins's physical strength and Lemon's gung-ho style, these grunts are human beings: they cuddle stockings as comforters and they are terrified of dentists.

Most of these traits and human characteristics, lastly, are also clearly suggested in the two short stories called "Enemies" and "Friends." What these two stories make very clear is that in the context of war, "normal" human behavior becomes more visible. Differently put, things that people's minds make them do in times of peace, they do even more fervently in times of war. In a fistfight over a missing jackknife Dave Jensen breaks Lee Strunk's nose; and as the narrator points out, "[i]n any other circumstance it might've ended there. But this was Vietnam, where guys carried guns, and Dave Jensen started to worry. *It was mostly in his head*" (67, emphasis added). But how this worry and fear of how Strunk might get back at him really turns his head is not made clear to the reader until s/he learns how one night Jensen borrows a pistol and "[uses] it like a hammer to break his own nose," and then asks Strunk "if things were square with them" (68). In the end, however, it turns out that it is not just Jensen who is a human being, feeling guilt over what he has done to his fellow soldier; Strunk himself admits that it was actually he who started it all: "'The man's crazy,' he said. 'I stole his fucking jackknife'" (68).

The importance of social codes and contracts, and how these are foregrounded in times of war, is stressed further in the follow-up story "Friends." Having now become buddies Jensen and Strunk make "a pact that if one of them should ever get totally fucked up—a wheelchair wound—the other guy would automatically find a way to end it" (71). But when Strunk loses a leg by stepping on a rigged mortar round, he goes crazy, not over the fact that his wound might kill him, but with fear that Jensen will stick to the contract. Jensen has to promise Strunk not to kill him as the latter is flown off to hospital. Even so, when Jensen learns in the end that Strunk has died, it seems "to relieve [him] of an enormous weight" (72).

To sum up, in the discussion above we have seen how these six stories, independently from the rest of the volume, communicate a number of important aspects of the Vietnam experience as envisioned by the implied author. (How they function in relation to the other stories of the volume will be discussed in the final section of this chapter.) The most important of these aspects is perhaps the *human* side of grunt life, because what these stories primarily deal with are basic human emotions, desires, and beliefs—such as superstition, embarrassment, guilt, and fear. What makes these short stories different from most of the longer stories in the volume, however, is the manner in which these emotions, and so on, are communicated to the reader. As we have seen, instead of making the reader identify with an often tragic protagonist, s/he is here presented with an outside perspective on an almost tragicomic character. In each of these stories, s/he is in a position to observe how the characters illustrate one or more of these emotions by committing some awkward final act. Perhaps the awkwardness of their acts—wearing an ex-girlfriend's stockings around one's neck, having a healthy tooth pulled, breaking one's own nose, and so on—is exactly what characterizes them as war experiences. It seems as if in war normal human behavior is put into clearer relief, as if everything becomes more visible. In "normal" daily life emotions like these can be hidden and contained by our personal defense mechanisms. But for foot soldiers in a war zone, where people live basically on top of each other and are constantly exposed to mental and physical hardships as well as the ever present threat of death, these emotions cannot be contained but are immediately acted out.

Here the narrator's final definition of a "true war story" comes to mind: "And in the end, of course, a true war story is never about war. [. . .] It's about [. . .] when you know you must [. . .] do things you are afraid to do" (91). As we have seen, this is exactly why Dobbins wears his girlfriend's stockings around his neck, why Lemon has a healthy tooth yanked out, and why Jensen breaks his nose—they are all afraid of something: going on ambush, showing embarrassment, meeting with retaliation, and so on.

Other Narrators

As we have seen, *Things* differs from the previous two texts in that the reader is presented with more than just one protagonist. A similarly important difference is that in *Things* the reader also listens to stories initially told by someone other than the narrator called "Tim O'Brien"; these "other" storytellers I will refer to as secondary narrators, as the regular narrator is still present to tell the story of how this other, metadiegetic, story was told. The other storytellers are primarily Mitchell Sanders in "How to Tell a True War Story" and "Night Life," and Rat Kiley in "Sweetheart of the Song Tra Bong"; but stories are also told by Jimmy Cross in "Love" and by Bowker in "Speaking of Courage" and "The Ghost Soldiers."

To illustrate the difference between a story told directly by the narrator and one which originates from a secondary narrator, and what this difference means to the role of the reader, let me refer to the old and new versions of "Night Life," the second to last story in the volume. Initially, this story was published as one of the "Six War Stories" discussed above. Just like these, "Night Life" illustrates what the enormous stress of the war could make the soldiers do. This time it is Rat who has had enough of what the grunts euphemistically call the "night life"; after two weeks of moving only in the dark due to enemy build-up, he cannot stand the strain anymore and commits the awkward act of shooting one of his toes off. The original version of "Night Life" shows its affinity to these other short war stories in that it has a similar communicative structure; that is, the narrator tells a story based on what he witnessed as a character:

> During those two weeks our basic routine was simple. We'd sleep away the daylight hours, or try to sleep, then at dusk we'd put on our gear and move out single file into the dark. ("Six War Stories" 104)

In other words, everything told is presented as personally witnessed by the narrator's younger self, the protagonist "Tim O'Brien."

In the version of the story presented in *Things*, however, the perspective of the protagonist as focalizer is exchanged for that of the character Sanders as secondary narrator. In keeping with this change the following lines were added as an introduction to the original story: "A few words about Rat Kiley. I wasn't there when he got hurt, but Mitchell Sanders later told me the essential facts. Apparently he lost his cool" (247). Hence, instead of hearing it firsthand, the reader in this new version is presented with a retelling of Sanders's story. As a consequence, the passage quoted above now reads:

> During those two weeks *the* basic routine was simple. *They'd* sleep away the daylight hours, or try to sleep, then at *dusk they'd* put on *their* gear and move out single file into the dark. (247–48, emphasis added)

In other words, the story of how Rat "lost his cool" has now turned into a third-person narrative. Another sign making it clear to the reader that the narrator has no personal experience of this specific event—an experience which instead should be attributed to Sanders—is the phrase "Sanders said," which is repeated no fewer than five times in the first three pages.

What, then, is the implied author's intent in changing his communicative strategy, and what are the consequences when it comes to the role of the reader? Read in isolation, or in the context of the other short war stories, it would seem that the original first-person perspective would provide the story with more authenticity; the event then appears to the reader to be something that the protagonist/narrator has witnessed with his own eyes. However, when the story is read as part of this volume—and as the second to last story of the volume—the situation is quite different. As we have seen, the reliability of the narrator as storyteller has been seriously undermined at this point in the reading process. So by transferring the responsibility for the happening-truth to Sanders, the implied author gives the reader less reason to doubt that this is exactly what happened to Rat Kiley. As it is now, it is Sanders who is the narrator's source for these "essential facts." In other words, the change of narrative strategy is a direct consequence of the change of textual context.

Whether or not Sanders is a more reliable source, however, is far from clear to the reader, we may assume. As we saw above in the discussion of the narrator's role as literary theorist in "How to Tell a True War Story," Sanders's story about the six men who go on a listening-post mission functions as an example of how a true war story always communicates a felt experience rather than the exact happening-truth. But although he sometimes had to make up a few things, Sanders is very anxious that his story is taken as truth; as the narrator comments: "I could tell how desperately Sanders wanted me to believe him, his frustration at not quite getting the details right, not quite pinning down the final and definite truth" (83); "He wanted me to feel the truth, to believe by the raw force of feeling" (81). As we have seen, comments of this kind on Sanders as secondary narrator tend to foreground the very act of storytelling itself, making the reader aware of the mechanisms behind a "true war story."

The story in which the act and mechanisms of storytelling are most clearly topicalized and exemplified, however, is "Sweetheart of the Song Tra Bong," in which Rat Kiley functions as secondary narrator. In the introduction to Rat's story, the narrator introduces him as a storyteller who had "a reputation for exaggeration and overstatement, a compulsion to rev up the facts." But, he lets the reader know, "[i]t wasn't a question of deceit. Just the opposite: he wanted to heat up the truth, to make it burn so hot that you *would feel exactly what he felt.* For Rat Kiley, I think, *facts were formed by sensation*, not the other way around" (101, emphasis added). In spite of this preliminary disclaimer, the narrator states that "with this particular story, Rat never backed down. He claimed to have witnessed the incident with his own eyes" (101–102).

What "sensation," or experience, is it then that Rat seeks to communicate in his story? Rat's "facts" are the following: "before joining Alpha Company, [he] had been assigned to a small medical detachment up in the mountains [...], near the village of Tra Bong" (102). One day, Fossie, one of the eight enlisted boys stationed there, brings his seventeen-year-old girlfriend, Mary Anne Bell, over to their lonely base in the jungle. Gradually, this sweet and innocent high-school girl becomes interested in the bloody work of the medics and in the war itself. She is drawn into the dark mystery and danger of combat. Eventually, she hooks up with a group of Special Forces, and one day she simply disappears into the jungle.

What these facts tell us, according to Rat, is that Mary Anne simply "got caught up in the Nam shit" (117). "What happened to her, Rat said, was what happened to all of them. You come over clean and you get dirty and then afterward it's never the same" (123). This means that, in principle, Mary Anne's experience is no different than the experience that they all have—a loss of innocence. The only difference is that here in Rat's story this particular experience is made clearer by substituting the usual young drafted soldier for an equally young and innocent girl. In other words, all Rat has done is to "rev up the facts" a little. So when she arrives on the helipad Rat has "[t]his cute blonde" dressed up in "[w]hite culottes and this sexy pink sweater"—the personification of innocence. But it is not only her initial state of innocence which is "revved up" in accordance with Rat's rhetoric of exaggeration; when she gets "caught up in the Nam shit," that is, when she loses her innocence, she is drawn into a kind of "heart of darkness." In a scene reminiscent of Conrad's story, Rat and Fossie find Mary Anne in the Greenies' candle-lit and incense-smelling hootch completely changed; not only does she now look like a typical Vietnam War veteran—"In part it was her eyes: utterly flat and indifferent. There was no emotion in her stare, no sense of person behind it"—she also appears to have donned the garb of evilness itself: "the grotesque part," says Rat, "was her jewelry At the girl's throat was a necklace of human tongues" (120). As Rat puts it, she seemed to be "lost inside herself". Having penetrated too deep "into the mystery of herself" (124), she could no longer stop the craving that had been awakened inside her:

> "Sometimes I want to eat this place. Vietnam. I want to swallow
> the whole country—the dirt, the death—I just want to eat it and
> have it there inside me. [...] When I'm out there at night, I feel

close to my own body, I can feel my blood moving, my skin and my fingernails, everything, it's like I'm full of electricity and I'm glowing in the dark—I'm on fire almost—I'm burning away into nothing—but it doesn't matter because I know exactly who I am. You can't feel like that anywhere else." (121)

Rat ends his story by simply stating that "one morning, all alone, Mary Anne walked off into the mountains and did not come back." It is suggested that she had "crossed to the other side" and was now "part of the land" (125).

We have thus seen how Rat manages to get his message—that anyone, no matter how innocent, can be corrupted by mere exposure to the Vietnam War—communicated to his narratees by "revving up" his facts. But how then is Rat's story itself presented to the reader? Briefly, the channels through which the implied author communicates with the reader in this story can be shown as in [the following table:]

Discourse level	Narrator	(Narratee)
Frame-story level	Rat (narrator)	Sanders (narratee)
		Protagonist (narratee/focalizer)
Object-story level	Rat (focalizer)	
	Mary Anne (main character)	

Narrative levels in "Sweetheart of the Song Tra Bong."

The way the implied author presents the story of Mary Anne is thus by having the narrator tell the story of how Rat used to tell this story, and specifically, how he once told it to Mitchell Sanders. This means that, at the frame-story level of "Sweetheart," Rat is telling his story to Sanders and the protagonist, the latter functioning also as focalizer since it is through his perspective that the event of the storytelling is perceived. At the object-story level, the reader is presented with the events of Rat's story, and at this level it is Rat, as a character in his own story, who functions as focalizer, as it is through his perception—"I saw it with my own eyes"—that the reader has access to what happened out at the Song Tra Bong.

In the text itself these levels of narration are clearly separated by a number of stylistic features. Whenever the reader's viewpoint is situated at the level of the frame story, Rat's narration is given as direct quotations within quotation marks. Moreover, in these passages Rat's act of narration is frequently commented on, both by Sanders and the narrator himself: "Rat's voice squeaked a little. He paused and looked at his hands" (102). Whenever the reader's viewpoint is moved down to the level of the object story, Rat's narration is rendered as a kind of free indirect discourse. At the beginning the primary narrator still uses a lot of reportive clauses—"As Rat described it, [...]" (103), or, "The way Rat told it, [...]" (105)—but the longer the viewpoint stays with the story of Mary Anne, the more independent the story appears to be from Rat as narrator. For long periods in the act of reading the reader is allowed to forget from whom this narration is emanating; the events are presented more or less as objective facts. In a few places, however, the narration is interrupted, and the reader's viewpoint is moved back up to the frame-story level, where the reader will hear Rat's frequent comments on, and interpretations of, the story, as well as Sanders's anger at Rat for breaking the spell of the story: "All these digressions, they just screw up your story's sound. Stick to what happened" (117).

The complex communicative setup of this story means that the reader has to construct two story worlds: one dominated by the perspective of the narrator and that of the protagonist as focalizer, and the other dominated by Rat's perspective, both as narrator and focalizer. The fact that the object story is situated at one remove from the narrator, suggesting that he cannot vouch for its truth, also means that the reader has to take into account Rat's "reputation for exaggeration and overstatement [...]," thus "performing rapid calculations in [his or her] head, subtracting superlatives, figuring the square root of an absolute and then multiplying by maybe" as most of Rat's narratees usually do. But whether or not the individual reader will believe Rat's story to be "true," s/he still has to be confronted with it at the level of the frame story—that is, s/he is exposed to a typical aspect of the Vietnam experience—that of being surrounded by "strange stories, some improbable, some well beyond that" (101). In other words, the implied author has situated the reader's viewpoint in the same position as Sanders and the protagonist, the narratees of Rat's story. Like the protagonist, the reader is seduced by Rat's story and taken to the deep jungles of Tra Bong in Rat's company; s/he is exposed to the problem of trying to take the character of Rat as narrator into account but at the same time finding him- or herself drawn into the world of the story, that is, the problem of what story to believe.

An indication of how important stories and storytelling are to the soldiers in Vietnam are the many critical objections that Sanders has to Rat's way of telling the story. He finds Rat's "tendency to stop now and then, interrupting the flow, inserting little clarifications or bits of analysis and personal opinion" to be a "bad habit" (116). Similarly, when Rat says he does not know what happened to Mary Anne in the end since he was transferred, Sanders goes crazy: "You can't do that," he tells Rat. "Jesus Christ, it's against the *rules* [...]. Against human *nature*. This elaborate story, you can't say, Hey, by the way, I don't know the *ending*. I mean, you got certain obligations" (122). So even though Rat does not know for sure what happened to Mary Anne—even though from now on it is "pure speculation"—Sanders forces him to "[f]inish up" (123)—to do what Paul Berlin does during his night of observation, "work out the possibilities." In other words, to leave a story unfinished is, according to the "rules" of the grunts, a much more serious offence than making things up. As we have seen before, stories have the function of creating some kind of order and certainty in a world "[w]here you can't tell where you are, or why you're there, and the only certainty is overwhelming ambiguity" (88).

To conclude, in the discussion above I have tried to show how, in the stories "Night Life," "How to Tell a True War Story," and "Sweetheart of the Song Tra Bong," the implied author chooses to make use of what might be termed secondary narrators in his attempt to communicate certain aspects of "O'Brien's" Vietnam experience. Through this strategy he forces the reader to listen to stories as they are being told, because the main difference between a primary and a secondary narrator is the respective perspectives they offer: the former is retrospective, the latter contemporary. Thus, by listening to a secondary narrator like Sanders or Rat, the reader is taken, not only to Vietnam, but from one place in Vietnam to another. In other words, the reader occupies the same position as the other grunts, the secondary narrator's narratees. From this position, the reader will *experience* what the protagonist experienced, rather than just be told about it. And what characterizes the protagonist's experience in these stories—especially in "Sweetheart"—as well as the reader's role in the text is a certain sense of ambiguity. Just like the protagonist, the reader faces the problem of what stories to believe: the narrator's story or Rat's story; one says don't trust Rat; the other says Rat tells the truth. Ultimately, it is up to each individual reader to try to bridge this gap.

Notes

13. In one instance the reader also has access to the thoughts of Kiowa, but not enough for us to call him a protagonist.

14. This is probably one of the reasons why this story is so often anthologized.

15. Tim O'Brien, "Introduction" to "Speaking of Courage." The exact same words are repeated in *Things* by the narrator in the succeeding postscript story, "Notes" (181).

16. Five of these stories—"Enemies," "Friends," "Stockings," "Church," and "The Dentist"—together with an earlier version of "Night Life" were published separately under the title *Six War Stories*.

DAVID R. JARRAWAY

"Excremental Assault" in Tim O'Brien:
Trauma and Recovery in Vietnam War Literature

"'You know something?'" [Azar] said. His voice was wistful. "'Out here,
at night, I almost feel like a kid again. The Vietnam experience. I mean,
wow, I *love* this shit.'"

—Tim O'Brien, *The Things They Carried*

"The excremental is all too intimately and inseparably bound up with the
sexual; the position of the genitals—*inter urinas et faeces*—remains the
decisive and unchangeable factor."

—Sigmund Freud, *Complete Letters*

"[Kathy Wade] remembered opening her robe to the humid night air.
There was a huge and desperate wanting in her heart, wanting without
object, pure wanting."

—Tim O'Brien, *In the Lake of the Woods*

"If at the end of a war story," Tim O'Brien writes in his second Vietnam
novel, *The Things They Carried* (1990), "you feel uplifted, or if you feel that
some small bit of rectitude has been salvaged from the larger waste, then
you have been made the victim of a very old and terrible lie" (*Things* 76).
O'Brien, of course, has not been the first to remark upon the larger waste
that is war. With reference to the Vietnam debacle in particular, Michael

From *Modern Fiction Studies* 44, no. 3 (Fall 1998): 695–711. Copyright © 1998 by the Purdue
Research Foundation.

Herr's *Dispatches* (1977) sets the tone for the wastage of that "psychotic vaudeville," as he calls it, almost from the beginning:

> [A] Marine came up to Lengle and me and asked if we'd like to look at some pictures he'd taken. . . . There were hundreds of these albums in Vietnam, thousands, and they all seemed to contain the same pictures. . . . the severed-head shot, the head often resting on the chest of the dead man or being held up by a smiling Marine, or a lot of heads, arranged in a row, with a burning cigarette in each of the mouths, the eyes open . . . a picture of a Marine holding an ear or maybe two ears or, as in the case of a guy I knew near Pleiku, a whole necklace made of ears, "love beads" as its owner called them; and the one we were looking at now, the dead Viet Cong girl with her pajamas stripped off and her legs raised stiffly in the air. (Herr 198–99)

In the face of such overwhelming madness, therefore, Tim O'Brien eradicates all possibility for responsive uplift in *The Things They Carried* by reducing even the metaphorical import of waste. As the measure of atrocious acts and imbecile events, waste's claim on all concerned, accordingly, is seen to be absolutely *literal*.

At this zero-degree level of rectitude, then, war becomes the equivalent of human waste—"a goddamn *shit* field" (*Things* 164)—in which an entire platoon must immerse itself in order to register most completely the nauseous vacuity and repulsive futility of their lives at war: "[A]fter a few days, the Song Tra Bong overflowed its banks and the land turned into a deep, thick muck for a half mile on either side. . . . Like quicksand, almost, except the stink was incredible. . . . You'd just sink in. You'd feel it ooze up over your body and sort of suck you down. . . . I mean, it never stopped, not ever" (161). "Finally somebody figured it out. What this was, it was. . . . The village toilet. No indoor plumbing, right? So they used the field" (164). "Rain and slop and shrapnel, it all mixed together, and the field seemed to boil . . . with the waste and the war" (191). "For twenty years," O'Brien's novel's narrator later remarks in hindsight, "this field had embodied all the waste that was Vietnam, all the vulgarity and horror" (210). That the full impact, however, of the "excremental assault" of my title should come to be realized so belatedly—*In Retrospect*, as Robert McNamara most recently puts forward the case—is, ironically, Vietnam's most extravagantly wasteful legacy.[1] But as one of O'Brien's least savory platoon members is given to remark, "'Eating shit—it's your classic irony'" (187).

Irony is the trope of trash or waste. And while it's not central to my purpose to trash or waste some of the more well-known literary theories endeavoring to come to terms with, if not indeed aiming to recover from, that extraordinarily riddling concatenation of events that is "Vietnam," I nonetheless want to cultivate a healthy sense of irony in an effort to disclose what discursive representations of war—theoretical as well as artistic—may actually be endeavoring to cover over or cover up—to re-cover, as it were.[2] The fiction of Tim O'Brien, *The Things They Carried* in particular, with its own healthy sense of irony, can gesture toward the shortcomings of theory. But, as I shall argue later, in keeping with that penetrating sense of irony even some of the best insights of *this* work may, too, have gone to waste, driving us on to O'Brien's next and most recent novel, *In the Lake of the Woods* (1994).

Kalí Tal, in her important essay "Speaking the Language of Pain," has been in the vanguard of a number of important writers to locate Vietnam literature in the context of the discourse of trauma.[3] In so doing, Tal underscores the chief failing of most literary theorists attempting to deal holistically with the war, namely, "their inevitable and total reduction of the war to metaphor" (Tal 223), whether this be the war's likeness to the myth-making of classic American literature (Philip Beidler), to the psychic landscape in literature closer to the present (John Hellman), or to the construction of the American self-image in the literature of the future (Thomas Myers).[4] As with all experiences of trauma (Holocaust literature, rape literature, incest literature, etc.), according to Tal, "Reality so violates personal mythologies" that only the example of "the literal immersion of concentration camp victims in shit ... of being forced to wear, eat, or swim in excrement"—only such "excremental assault" (a phrase she borrows from Terrance Des Pres's *The Survivor: An Anatomy of Life in the Death Camps* [1976])—can approximate the individual's totally abject sense of psychic and social "violation" (Tal 234). Yet the transformation of national or cultural myths is dependent organically upon the revision of personal myths (Tal 243). Hence, any kind of real social or cultural amelioration envisioned in mythically discursive terms is most likely to occur as a consequence of trauma, whose excremental horror "strike[s] at the very core of the victim's conception of self in the world, forcing the most radical restructuring of personal myth ... to include the previously unthinkable" (234).[5]

What Tal, however, is insistent upon throughout her essay is the almost impossible task to which the trauma author becomes heir. "For if the goal is to convey the traumatic experience," as she explains, "no secondhand rendering of it is adequate. The horrific events which have reshaped the author's construction of reality can only be described [and] not re-created" (Tal 231). Thus, the trauma author appears forever to be laboring in a "liminal state," a kind of "unbridgeable gap between writer and reader" (218) that is bounded, on the one side, by "the urge to bear witness, to carry the tale of horror back to the halls of normalcy" (229), and on the other, by "the truth of the experience" that "in even the most powerful writing ... language cannot reach or explicate" (222). Working at cross-purposes in this way, the trauma author is rather like O'Brien's Lieutenant Jimmy Cross in *The Things They Carried*, never quite succeeding in having his men "get their shit together, . . . keep it together, and maintain it neatly and in good working order" (*Things* 24).[6]

The closest experience, therefore, that we as readers of Vietnam literature are ever likely to have that might approximate something of its trauma will undoubtedly lie, along with its authors, in that "liminal state" between what we may already know too well, and what we sense is hardly there for us to imagine. The two senses of "re-covery" in my title noted previously thus speak to both sides of trauma's liminal divide. Georges Bataille, who perhaps knows more about excremental assault than most, in his *Visions of Excess* gives us the initial sense of a calculated recovery, usually in closed forms of discourse whose economy, in the end, "is limited to reproduction and to the conservation of human life" (116). In more open forms of discourse, however, whose economy of "unproductive expenditure" is likely to include the traumas of "war" and "perverse sexual activity" (118), we have the quite other sense of a more radical form of recovery since expenditure, as revealed in its "excremental symbolism," is mainly "directed toward loss" rather than "the principle of conservation" and the "stability of fortunes" (122).

Recovery from trauma, then, in this more radical form can only proceed, as Tal suggests, by way of a restructuring of personal experience in a wholly *expendable* way. In contrast, the more conservative notion of recovery, by falling back upon the already known and familiar, will negate the reality of trauma by failing to include in personal experience what has been formerly left unthought. And yet the temptation to collapse the former sense of recovery into the latter, in effect, *to cover up* the trauma that is Vietnam, would appear to be overwhelming, as that horror is strikingly rendered in *The Things They Carried*:

> For the common soldier, at least, war has the feel—the spiritual texture—of a great ghostly fog, thick and permanent. There is no clarity. Everything swirls. The old rules are no longer binding, the old truths no longer true. Right spills over into wrong. Order blends into chaos, love into hate, ugliness into beauty, law into anarchy, civility into savagery. The vapors suck you in. You can't tell where you are, or why you're there, and the only certainty is overwhelming ambiguity. In war you lose your sense of the definite, hence your sense of truth itself, and therefore it's safe to say that in a true war story nothing is ever absolutely true. (88)

Nonetheless, O'Brien, like Bataille, will hew to that loss of the definite, and elsewhere insist on the war's "uncertainty" (*Things* 44), its "mystery" (209), and what he candidly admits is sometimes "just beyond telling" (79).[7] For if there is to be any kind of recovery from the trauma that promises no more Vietnams, only the kind of openness and responsiveness to experience that can make what is "absolutely true" quite expendable will do. In place of a character like Rat Kiley whose obsession with "policing up the parts" and "plugging up holes" (249–50) ultimately leads to his turning his own gun on himself as the surefire method of withstanding change, O'Brien perhaps suggests something more redemptive in the example of an unknown soldier waist-deep back in the shit field: "Bent forward at the waist, groping with both hands, he seemed to be chasing some creature just beyond reach, something elusive, a fish or a frog" (192). Bataille, in a passage that elucidates O'Brien's description of the shit field, writes: "[T]he moment when the ordered and reserved . . . lose themselves for ends that cannot be subordinated to anything one can account for" is precisely that moment when "life starts" (Bataille 128).

Life starts for both the authors and readers of Vietnam literature in those moments when the most authentic form of recovery in the trauma text represents a groping after the unaccountable, the unthinkable, and the unsayable. In the space remaining, I will dwell on three such exemplary moments in O'Brien's work—moments in which the excremental assault of war proves to be almost insupportable. In each case, nothing less than a wholly new conceptualization of subjectivity is called for—a "traumatic moment of epiphany," as it were (Žižek 34). And the recovery's success will largely depend upon the degree to which, translating Tal in the terms of both Bataille and O'Brien, the radical restructuring of personal myth will be carried forward in the direction of "things" that cannot be subordinated to anything one can discursively account for.

My first example of a promised recovery occurs, predictably enough, exactly at that moment, in the "Sweetheart of the Song Tra Bong" chapter of O'Brien's *Things*, when the character involved disappears at its end: "She [Mary Anne Bell] had crossed to the other side. She was part of the land. . . . She was dangerous. She was ready for the kill" (125). Mary Anne is the seventeen-year-old girlfriend of Mark Fossie whom he secretly flies from Cleveland to Vietnam to keep him company between battle maneuvers. Scandalously out of place in the battlefield, Mary Anne nonetheless is for a time tolerated by platoon members to the extent that she confirms their sexist myths of the active and aggressive male and the passive and docile female in cultures both home and abroad: "The way she looked, Mary Anne made you think about those girls back home, how clean and innocent they all are, how they'll never understand any of this, not in a billion years" (123).

But very quickly, Mary Anne becomes immersed in the excremental assault of war first hand—"She was up to her eyeballs in it," Rat Kiley acerbically remarks (*Things* 123)—and as a result, gradually begins to alter her sense of self by forming new attachments to the Green Berets, undertaking to assist medically in the fields of combat, and eventually embroiling herself directly in ambush operations, sometimes for weeks at a stretch. The "new confidence in her voice, [and] new authority in the ways she carried herself" (109), in the end, instructively reveals that the trauma of wartime liminality—"that mix of unnamed terror and unnamed pleasure" (123)[8]—can sometimes prove to have beneficial consequences, provided, as Rat Kiley ironically observes, that "you know you're risking something":

> [Y]ou become intimate with danger; you're in touch with the far side of yourself, as though it's another hemisphere, and you want to string it out and go wherever the trip takes you and be host to all the possibilities inside yourself. Not *bad*, she'd said. Vietnam made her glow in the dark. She wanted more, she wanted to penetrate deeper into the mystery of herself, and after a time the wanting became needing, which turned then to craving. . . . She was lost inside herself. (124)

In losing her self, echoing Bataille, to a host of possibilities not restricted in any sense to the essentializing exclusiveness of culturally approbated gender roles, trauma thus moves Mary Anne into that healthful space that "cannot be condensed into a 'proper locus,'" to borrow the phrasing of Elspeth Probyn, and where the self finds its recovery "as a theoretical manoeuvering, not as a unifying principle" (106). And if Mary Anne Bell disappears at the end of her chapter, it's only because, like Kathy Wade in O'Brien's next novel, *In the Lake of the Woods*, she enters into that permanent state of missing persons where "Mystery finally claims us all" (*In the Lake* 304).

My second unspeakably traumatic moment that promises recovery through subjective enlargement occurs in "The Ghost Soldiers" chapter of *The Things They Carried*, when the narrator is wounded from behind, and narrowly escapes death from the incompetent ministrations of an inexperienced medic terrified by battle:

> So when I got shot the second time, in the butt, along the Song Tra Bong, it took the son of a bitch ten minutes to work up the nerve to crawl over to me. By then I was gone with the pain. Later I found out I'd almost died of shock. To make it worse, [the medic]

bungled the patch job, and a couple of weeks later my ass started
to rot away. . . . It was borderline gangrene. I spent a month flat on
my stomach; I couldn't walk or sit; I couldn't sleep. . . . After the rot
cleared up, once I could think straight, I devoted a lot of time to
figuring ways to get back at him. (*Things* 218)

In this passage, what is perhaps more insupportable for the narrator than his
weeks of agonizing pain recuperating in a foreign hospital is his enforced
removal from a community of men whose fierce loyalty and compassion for
each other the shock of war is able to authenticate in any number of pas-
sionately charged ways—homosocial possibilities somewhat ironically belied
by the narrator's vengeful intention merely to "think straight." When the
worst thing that Vietnam can do for you is "[turn] you sentimental," and
"[make] you want to hook up with girls like Mary Hopkin" (235), when
the "sense of pure and total loss" in wartime comes down to finding you
"didn't fit [in] anymore" (225) with "guys" who "loved one another" (221),
abandoning you to "dark closets, madmen, [and] murderers" (231), when
even "the clean, sterile smell of [your] rear" can suggest an insupportable
"sense of separation" (221) from other men in comparison to "the awful
stink of [yourself]" (227)—all of this homoerotic "double talk," in Wayne
Koestenbaum's phrase opens up an unspeakable hole in the trauma text into
which Freud may have been reluctant to insert his finger (Koestenbaum
30),[9] but which the narrator of *The Things They Carried* shows no hesitation
about penetrating:

I remembered lying there for a long while, listening to the river,
the gunfire and voices, how I kept calling out for a medic but how
nobody came and how I finally came and how I finally reached
back and touched the hole. The blood was warm like dishwater. I
could feel my pants filling up with it. All this blood, I thought—
I'll be *hollow.* Then the brittle sensation hit me. I passed out. . . .
(*Things* 238)

The extraordinary tension in this passage between abject physical pain
and a kind of orgasmic pleasure—"how nobody came" and "how I finally
came"—gives considerable weight to O'Brien's previous remark about the
only certainty being the overwhelming ambiguity of war. But the ambiguity
is there, I think, at least to enlist the possibility of legitimating notions of
queer subjectivity in contexts previously unspeakable, so that for one traumatic moment, as O'Brien puts it, "the whole comrade business gets turned
around" (*Things* 221).[10]

Koestenbaum observes that "[a]nal secrets filled many of Freud's letters to [Wilhelm] Fliess" (36), not the least among which in that homoerotic correspondence is Freud's excitement over "all the things that resolve themselves into—excrement for me (a new Midas!)" (Freud qtd. in Koestenbaum 36). Daniel Boyarin, more recently, has made explicit even further Freud's "association between the anus, anal penetration, shit, and birth-giving," singling out Freud's "excrement babies" as "the necessary condition of sexual satisfaction from a man" (127). What we learn of the excremental privileging of anal sexuality in an early phase of psychoanalytic discourse can perhaps suggest a good deal about O'Brien's own preoccupation with the imagery of waste from the standpoint of trauma's gross re-visioning of personal and national ideologies that the recent controversy over gays in the military, for example, has only slightly begun to gesture toward.

And central to the radical recovery of anality, within a psychoanalytic revisionism at any rate, is the need to give some credence, as Boyarin writes, to the "homoerotic desire . . . for 'femaleness,' for passivity, to be the object of another man's desire, even to bear the child of another man" (129). So that when the whole comrade business gets turned around, as O'Brien puts it, it might be possible at last to "stare into the big black hole at the center of your own sorry soul" (*Things* 231), much like Mary Anne previously, and discover not the usual "candy-asses" (21) looking to escape the war, or the "damned sissy . . . taken off for Canada" (48), or even the "pussy for president" who might put an end to war (117), but a man who can transcend the homophobia compounded by misogyny in mainstream culture by *the very fact* of his femininity:

> Frail-looking, delicately boned, the young man had never wanted to be a soldier and in his heart had feared that he would perform badly in battle. . . . He had no stomach for violence. He loved mathematics. His eyebrows were thin and arched like a woman's, and at school the boys sometimes teased him about how pretty he was, the arched eyebrows and long shapely fingers, and on the playground they would mimic a woman's walk and make fun of his smooth skin and his love for mathematics. He could not make himself fight them. (142)

Eventually, this young man will go off to war, and become the single Vietnamese victim of the narrator himself. And his senseless death will prompt the narrator, twenty years later, to return with his young daughter to Vietnam, to immerse himself in what was once the shit field of the Song Tra Bong, and bury the hatchet of a fallen Native American comrade named Kiowa, as an act of reparation and penance for the murder of a man who just possibly might have been the object of the narrator's own desire, if not enduring love.

Still, that rather pat resolution to a quite extraordinary sequence of homosexual tensions throughout *The Things They Carried* might suggest that the work of trauma, most active in its intractable liminality, may itself have been too easily buried in the waste of war, if the irony of Rat Kiley's "plugging up holes" (not to mention the narrator's own anal wound) is at all significant. But perhaps it's O'Brien's own fixation on his victim's eyes—"one eye was shut and the other was a star-shaped hole" (*Things* 140)—where we catch sight of trauma's unfinished business. "I imagined the eye at the summit of the skull," Bataille writes, "like a horrible erupting volcano ... associated with the rear end and its excretions" (74). The excremental assault fomented by Bataille's pineal eye/solar anus in *Visions of Excess*, so like the "star-shaped hole" of the narrator's victim, will thus have to be resumed in O'Brien's next novel, where John Wade's loss to "the tangle" of selfhood will find an appropriate extension in Wade's desire "to crawl into a hole" (*In the Lake* 296), and disappear like his wife before him. "[T]he eye can only be opened when another eye is closed," is Lee Edelman's extrapolation from a parallel vision of anal desire in Freud ("Piss Elegant" 153; see also 173), which seems to fit the relation between O'Brien's two novels almost precisely.[11]

My final example of trauma, therefore, argues for a kind of ironic recovery somewhere between the success of Mary Anne Bell earlier, and the failure of O'Brien's narrator later.[12] It occurs in the "Speaking of Courage" chapter of *Things* when Norman Bowker, surprised by sudden mortar fire one dark night, discovers that his friend Kiowa has been swallowed up completely by the waste of the swampy battlefield, and for a split second, experiences a failure of nerve: "[H]ow he had taken hold of Kiowa's boot and pulled hard, but how the smell was simply too much, and how he'd backed off and in that way had lost the Silver Star" (*Things* 172):

> [A]nd then suddenly he felt himself going too. He could taste it. The shit was in his nose and eyes ... and the stink was everywhere—it was inside his lungs—and he could no longer tolerate it. Not here, he thought. Not like this ... and then he lay still and tasted the shit in his mouth and closed his eyes and listened to the rain and explosions and bubbling sounds. ... A good war story, he thought, but it was not a war for war stories, nor for talk of valor, and nobody in town wanted to know about the terrible stink. They wanted good intentions and good deeds. (168–69)

From that day forward, and for several years thereafter back in Des Moines, Norman Bowker relives that moment of weakness in his father's Chevy by driving it endlessly around a nearby lake, his carefully timed seven-mile orbits performing a kind of expiation for letting down his buddy, for falling woefully short of the expectations of his father and townsfolk, but mostly for failing the promise within himself.

Bowker's car circling the lake thus becomes a powerful metaphor not only for revolving the excremental trauma of war in its suggestive displacement onto the equally punishing domestic contexts of family and community back home—"a nucleus" around which O'Brien, in his following "Notes" chapter, would suggest his entire novel turns (*Things* 180). But Bowker's endless circling also brings round once again both the self-preserving and the self-denying forms of recovery at the very catastrophic center of the literature of witness. "In combat," as Judith Herman observes, "witnessing the death of a buddy places the soldier at particularly high risk for developing posttraumatic stress disorder" (54).[13] Three years after Norman Bowker's chapter ends, so the narrator informs us, Bowker commits suicide, an act he seems already to anticipate—"suddenly he felt himself going too"—by relaxing his tolerance for an unfamiliar and fearful circumstance, at the very moment when all of his tenacity and resourcefulness to deal with the shock of the new are needed. Ironically, in saving his own life, he ultimately loses it. Yet those endless repetitions centered on that lake back in Iowa suggest that Bowker is in on the game at quite a different level: a perverse kind of Lacanian "enjoyment" betokened by "the circular movement which finds *satisfaction* in failing again and again to attain the object" (Žižek 48; emphasis added). On that level, the expenditure of effort is not directed toward any self-serving end, but (as in a quite similar Lake of the Woods in O'Brien's next work, "where all is repetition") rather than fall back, one moves forward to a much larger although as yet imperfectly known vision of selfhood, motored, like Kathy Wade, only by "a huge and desperate wanting in her heart, wanting without object, pure wanting" (*In the Lake* 257).

In the end, I'm tempted to argue that the liminality of Bowker's knowing just enough to understand practically nothing about himself makes him the ideal witness to trauma.[14] And for the ideal readers of Vietnam literature, he continues to remain, like John Wade in *In the Lake of the Woods*, a little "beyond knowing": "We are fascinated, all of us, by the implacable otherness of others. And we wish to penetrate by hypothesis, by day-dream, by scientific investigation those leaden walls that encase the human spirit, that define it and guard it and hold it forever inaccessible" (103). "I prowl and smoke cigarettes. I review my notes. The truth is at once simple and baffling: John Wade was a pro. He did his magic, then walked away. Everything else is conjecture. No answers, yet mystery itself carries me on" (269). This concluding reference to a driving mystery—"a mystery that is simply the world of the beyond" (Caruth, *Unclaimed* 145 n.15)—perhaps yields the ultimate irony of Tim O'Brien's work, given his stated intention, in a recent *New York Times* interview, "to stop writing fiction for the foreseeable future" ("Doing" 33). This mystery may not be a bad thing, if our attention is diverted back to so much else that awaits us in the discourse of trauma, where the mysteries of recovery more properly lie. "The Vietnam experience," as one character from *Things* cryptically attests, "I mean, wow, I *love* this shit" (237).

NOTES

1. Indeed, the "belated" recognition of the significance of the whole "Vietnam" experience forms a chief aspect of its conceptualization in the context of psychic trauma as I attempt to locate it here. As Cathy Caruth observes in *Unclaimed Experience*, "Traumatic experience, beyond the psychological dimension of suffering it involves, suggests a certain paradox: that the most direct seeing of a violent event may occur as an absolute inability to know it; that immediacy, paradoxically, may take the form of belatedness" (92).

2. Thus, as Tina Chen recently observed, "O'Brien's stories are not about recovering from trauma or resolving the conflicts contributing to or created by the war in any permanent way; they are about accepting indeterminacy and learning to live not through Vietnam but with it" (80).

3. Of the three broad experiences of trauma dealt with in her important *Trauma and Recovery*, namely hysteria, shell shock, and sexual abuse (Herman 9), Judith Herman deals with the particular instance of "Vietnam" throughout her study under the second heading, and refers to O'Brien's *Things* as a leading instance (see 38, 52, 137). For similar treatments of the Vietnam experience in this psychomedical context, see also Kulka et al., Lifton, and Figley and Levantman.

4. Kalí Tal references her comments specifically to Philip Beidler's *American Literature and the Experience of Vietnam* (1982), John Hellman's *American Myth and the Legacy of Vietnam* (1986), and Thomas Myers's *Walking Point: American Narratives of Vietnam* (1988), among other important theoretical works that tend to totalize the experience of the Vietnam War (Tal 218–23).

5. In Lacanian terms, the most radical restructuring of subjective "myth," as Slavoj Žižek points out, "triggering a traumatic crackup of our psychic balance," will come from the direction of the Real as "the previously unthinkable," hence "alien to the symbolic order" (11)—the "life substance [ironically] that proves a shock for the symbolic universe" (22). "What ultimately interrupts the continuous flow of words, what hinders the smooth running of the symbolic circuit, is the traumatic presence of the Real: when the words stay out, we have to look not for imaginary resistances but for the object that came too close" (23)—"an objectival remainder—excrement" (43). Caruth also alludes to the Lacanian address in Žižek to theorize trauma as "an 'escape' from the real into ideology" (*Unclaimed* 142 n. 9). Žižek also insightfully remarks that suicide is often at the center of subjectivity's encounter with the Real, an important aspect of O'Brien's *Things* that I shall return to later. But on the duplicitous (rather than salubrious) sense of "recovery" just scanned, Žižek notes that we often notice in acts of suicide "a desperate attempt to recover the traumatic encounter of the Real . . . by means of integrating it into a symbolic universe of guilt,

locating it within an ideological field, and thus conferring meaning upon it" (42). This last idea will gradually become clearer as we proceed.

6. On language's inablility to "explicate" the trauma of war just noted, Caruth, in her important collection of essays on the subject, remarks generally upon "the way [traumatic experience] *escapes* full consciousness as it occurs," that it "cannot, as Georges Bataille says, become a matter of 'intelligence,'" and that "it seems to evoke the difficult truth of a history that is constituted by the very incomprehensibility of its occurrence" ("Recapturing" 153).

7. I have discussed these aspects of the Vietnam conflict at some length previously in "'Standing by His Word': The Politics of Allen Ginsberg's Vietnam 'Vortex.'" For a further expansion of the Vietnam experience in the context of trauma as a "crisis of truth" and "a crisis of evidence," see Felman 17 and passim.

8. O'Brien's phrase here comes remarkably close to Žižek's unpacking of Lacan's trauma-discourse: "even if the psychic apparatus is entirely left to itself, it will not attain the balance for which the 'pleasure principle' strives, but will continue to circulate around a traumatic intruder in its interior. . . . [T]he Lacanian name for this 'pleasure in pain' is of course enjoyment (*jouissance*) . . . the circular movement [of] which finds satisfaction in failing again and again to attain the object" (48). For the liminal "inbetweenness" of the traumatic experience, Caruth looks before Lacan to Freud, where the "temporal definition of trauma in *Beyond the Pleasure Principle* seems to be an extension of his early understanding of trauma as being locatable not in one moment alone but in the relation between two moments . . . [in] the description of the traumatic experience in terms of its temporal unlocatability" (*Unclaimed* 133 n. 8).

9. Freud's English translator, James Strachey, wrote in a footnote: "At this point (so Freud told the present editor, with his finger on an open copy of the book) there is a hiatus in the text [of Josef Breuer and Freud's collaboration, *Studies on Hysteria*, wherein the hysterical childbirth of Anna O. had been deliberately omitted by Breuer]" (qtd. in Koestenbaum 29). Comments Koestenbaum: "Anna's unmentionable pseudo-motherhood is the hole in Breuer's text; her pregnancy is as unspeakable as the hole in Breuer where Freud inserts his 'finger,' filling up a space that the elder [Breuer] modestly (and flagrantly) leaves open. Leaving holes in his text is Breuer's style of seduction: these blanks encourage Freud's participation" (29–30). Caruth follows Henry Krystal in underscoring trauma as a kind of psychic discourse in which "a void, a hole is found" ("Traumatic" 6).

10. O'Brien's wordplay on "whole" in this passage yields a further means of comprehending the traumatic Real in the context of subjective enlargement, setting us as it does before "[a]n identification with what psychoanalysis calls the 'anal object,' a remainder, an amorphous leftover of some harmonious Whole [for which] Lacan quotes Luther's sermons: 'You are the excrement which fell on the earth through the Devil's anus'" (Žižek 178). Comments Žižek, "[W]hat we have here is the opposition between a harmonious work of art ["straight" readings of O'Brien's novel, perhaps?] and the queer remainder which sticks out" (179).

11. Edelman secures several extraordinary intertextual linkages between Freud and Alfred Hitchcock on the eye as an image of anal desire in the manner of Bataille, and one instance in particular, occurring at the end of Hitchcock's *Psycho*, sets up an uncanny resonance with O'Brien's text on this issue: "But [the film] cannot (a)void the end to which its narrative logic compels it: a vision of the swamp as toilet, as the cavernous place of shit, disclosing the back end of Marion's car, like the eye that emerged from the drain, and with it the winking caption that names this

site of waste as 'the end'" ("Piss Elegant" 165). Hence, the problematic of "plugging up holes" in the unfinished business of O'Brien's decidedly anal-oriented text noted previously forms an instructive intersection with Edelman's own conclusion: "Thus Freud, like Hitchcock or like Norman Bates, dreamed of exchanging an eye for an eye, of voiding the telltale stain of the anus staring back from every hole. . . . [Yet,] 'it is not easy for anyone to serve two masters' . . .—insofar, that is, as [normalization] seeks to shut that eye by plugging the anal hole, must only stage anew the vision of anal desire and guarantee the blind logic of its inevitable return" ("Piss Elegant" 173).

12. If irony is the trashy trope of trauma, noted earlier, then in the context of the *fuller* recovery of selfhood in O'Brien's fiction, Paul de Man is enormously instructive on its rhetorical deployments when he asserts, "Irony comes into being when self-consciousness loses its control over itself. For me, at least, the way I think of it now, irony is not a figure of self-consciousness. It's a break, an interruption, a disruption. It is a moment of loss of control, and not just for the author but for the reader as well" (qtd. in Edelman, *Homographesis* 225).

13. Herman further elaborates:

> Hendin and Haas found in their study of combat veterans with post-traumatic stress disorder ["Suicide and Guilt Manifestation of PTSD in Vietnam Combat Veterans"] that a significant minority had made suicide attempts (19 percent) or were constantly preoccupied with suicide (15 percent). Most of the men who were persistently suicidal had had heavy combat exposure. They suffered from unresolved guilt about their wartime experiences and from severe, unremitting anxiety, depression, and post-traumatic symptoms. Three of the men died by suicide during the course of the study. (50)

What is more, "Caught in a political conflict that should have been resolved before their lives were placed at risk, returning soldiers often felt traumatized a second time when they encountered public criticism and rejection of the war they had fought and lost" (71).

14. Claude Lanzmann, in his essay-contribution to *Trauma: Explorations in Memory*, cites Lacan precisely to the same effect: "[O]ne of the things which we should be watching out for most, is not to understand too much, not to understand more than what there is in the discourse of the subject. . . . I will even say that it is on the basis of a certain refusal of understanding that we open the door onto psychoanalytic understanding" (qtd. in Lanzmann 204).

WORKS CITED

Bataille, Georges. *Visions of Excess: Selected Writings, 1927–1939*. Ed. Allan Stoekl. Trans. Allan Stoekl, Carl R. Lovitt, and Donald M. Leslie, Jr. Theory and History of Literature 14. Minneapolis: U of Minnesota P, 1985.

Boyarin, Daniel. "Freud's Baby, Fliess's Maybe: Homophobia, Anti–Semitism, and the Invention of Oedipus." *Pink Freud*. Ed. Diana Fuss. Spec. issue of *GLQ: A Journal of Lesbian and Gay Studies* 2.1–2 (1995): 115–47.

Caruth, Cathy. *Unclaimed Experience: Trauma, Narrative, and History*. Baltimore: Johns Hopkins UP, 1996.

———. Introduction. "Recapturing the Past." *Trauma: Explorations in Memory* 151–57.

———. Introduction. "Traumatic Experience." *Trauma: Explorations in Memory* 3–12.

———, ed. *Trauma: Explorations in Memory.* Baltimore: Johns Hopkins UP, 1995.

Chen, Tina. "'Unraveling the Deeper Meaning': Exile and the Embodied Poetics of Displacement in Tim O'Brien's *The Things They Carried.*" *Contemporary Literature* 39.1 (1998): 77–98.

Edelman, Lee. "Piss Elegant: Freud, Hitchcock, and the Micturating Penis." *Pink Freud.* Ed. Diana Fuss. Spec. issue of *GLQ: A Journal of Lesbian and Gay Studies* 2.1–2 (1995): 149–77.

———. *Homographesis: Essays in Gay Literary and Cultural Theory.* New York: Routledge, 1994.

Felman, Shoshana. "Education and Crisis, or the Vicissitudes of Teaching." *Trauma: Explorations in Memory* 13–60.

Figley, C., and Levantman, S., eds. *Strangers at Home: Vietnam Veterans Since the War.* New York: Praeger, 1980.

Freud, Sigmund. *The Complete Letters of Sigmund Freud to Wilhelm Fliess, 1887–1904.* Ed. and trans. Jeffrey Moussaieff Masson. Cambridge: Harvard UP, 1985.

Herman, Judith Lewis. *Trauma and Recovery.* New York: Basic, 1997.

Herr, Michael. *Dispatches.* New York: Avon, 1978.

Jarraway, David R. "'Standing by His Word': The Politics of Allen Ginsberg's Vietnam 'Vortex.'" *Journal of American Culture* 16.3 (1993): 81–88.

Koestenbaum, Wayne. *Double Talk: The Erotics of Male Literary Collaboration.* New York, Routledge, 1989.

Kulka, R. A., et al. *Trauma and the Vietnam War Generation.* New York: Brunner/Mazel, 1990.

Lanzmann, Claude. "The Obscenity of Understanding: An Evening with Claude Lanzmann." *Trauma: Explorations in Memory* 200–20.

Lifton, R. J. *Home from the War: Vietnam Veterans: Neither Victims nor Executioners.* New York: Simon, 1973.

Myers, Thomas. *Walking Point: American Narratives of Vietnam.* New York: Oxford University Press, 1988.

O'Brien, Tim. Interview. "Doing the Popular Thing." *The New York Times Book Review* 9 Oct. 1994: 33.

———. *In the Lake of the Woods.* Boston: Houghton, 1994.

———. *The Things They Carried.* Boston: Houghton, 1990.

Probyn, Elspeth. *Sexing the Self: Gendered Positions in Cultural Studies.* New York: Routledge, 1993.

Tal, Kalí. "Speaking the Language of Pain: Vietnam War Literature in the Context of a Literature of Trauma." *Fourteen Landing Zones: Approaches to Vietnam War Literature.* Ed. Philip K. Jason. Iowa City: U of Iowa P, 1991. 217–50.

Žižek, Slavoj. *Enjoy Your Symptom! Jacques Lacan in Hollywood and Out.* New York: Routledge, 1992.

JIM NEILSON

Undying Uncertainty

Tim O'Brien is probably the best known and most acclaimed novelist of
the Vietnam War. His *Going After Cacciato* won the National Book Award,
and *The Things They Carried* was a finalist for both the Pulitzer Prize and
the National Book Critics Circle Award. Robert Harris in the *New York
Times Book Review* places the latter not merely on "the short list of essential
fiction about Vietnam" but "high up on the list of best fiction about *any*
war." To Peter Prescott in *Newsweek*, two or three stories in *The Things
They Carried* "seem as good as any short stories written about any war." And
Michiko Kakutani in the daily *New York Times* declares *The Things They
Carried* "a vital, important book—a book that matters."[1]

The Things They Carried is a hybrid text, a collection of stories that functions as a novel. Characters and incidents are repeated from story to story and
are refracted through several literary modes and through the O'Brien narra-
tor/persona's shifting self-interest and self-delusion. An embodiment of the
processive and indeterminate nature of consciousness, *The Things They Carried* replicates a veteran's struggle to make sense of wartime experience and
memory. It is at once a recounting of a soldier's experiences in Vietnam and
an interrogation of how such experiences are transformed into fiction by the
imagination, as can be seen in one of the novel's central incidents—the death
of O'Brien's comrade Kiowa.

From *Warring Fictions: American Literary Culture and the Vietnam War Narrative*, pp. 192–209.
Copyright © 1998 by University Press of Mississippi.

In the story "Speaking of Courage," O'Brien tells us his platoon biv-ouacked beside the Song Tra Bong River in what they discovered too late was "a shit field. The village toilet" (164). Rain transformed this field into "deep, oozy soup. . . . Like sewage" (164). During the night the platoon was bombarded by mortar fire that made the ground explode and boil. When Kiowa began to drown in this shit field, another soldier, Norman Bowker, "grabbed Kiowa by the boot and tried to pull him out. . . . then suddenly he felt himself going too. He could taste it. The shit was in his nose and eyes. . . . and he could no longer tolerate it. . . . He released Kiowa's boot and watched it slide away" (168). O'Brien repeatedly forces this image before us to convey the horror of war. It also serves as a metaphor for combat: to American soldiers in Vietnam "the shit" referred to "the day-to-day com-bat operations endured by GIs in the field" (Clark, 463). O'Brien revivifies this conventional metaphor by making it horribly tangible. That men's lives were wasted in Vietnam is likewise emblematized by the shit field. Kiowa's death also evokes the notion that for the U.S. Vietnam was a quagmire; his drowning functions almost emblematically to suggest America's deepening entanglement in southeast Asia. "This field," O'Brien writes, "had embodied all the waste that was Vietnam" (210).

What is striking about *The Things They Carried*, though, is not O'Brien's use of metaphor but his elaborate and elusive self-consciousness. He gives us several versions of this incident and foregrounds his role in shaping these sto-ries. In "Speaking of Courage," he tells us that Norman Bowker failed to save Kiowa. In "Notes," he reveals that Kiowa's death had been omitted from an earlier version of this story and that Bowker, haunted by that night, had com-mitted suicide. In another story, "In the Field," O'Brien blames not Bowker but an unnamed soldier who instigated the mortar attack by carelessly turn-ing on his flashlight. And in "Field Trip" O'Brien tells us about his return to the site of Kiowa's death years after the war. "That little field," he writes, "had swallowed so much. My best friend. My pride. My belief in myself as a man of some small dignity and courage. Still, it was hard to find any real emotion. . . . After that long night in the rain, I'd seemed to grow cold inside, all the illusions gone, all the old ambitions and hopes for myself sucked away into the mud" (210). Nowhere in *The Things They Carried* does O'Brien explain more clearly the psychic devastation wrought by wartime trauma. In order to overcome this trauma and to regain what he lost in Kiowa's death, he must confront his past, so he wades into the filthy river. Previously, O'Brien had "felt a certain smugness about how easily [he] had made the shift from war to peace" (179). Now he writes, "in a way . . . I'd gone under with Kiowa, and . . . after two decades I'd finally worked my way out. . . . I felt something go shut in my heart while something else swung open" (212).

O'Brien's intensity here and in his many other attempts to come to terms with his battlefield experiences suggests how important it is for him to tell the truth about what happened in Vietnam. Indeed, in a story entitled "How to Tell a True War Story," he repeatedly points to the accuracy of his fiction: "This is true" (75), be writes, "It's all exactly true" (77), "It all happened" (83), "here's what actually happened" (85). But such repeated insistence upon the truthfulness of his fiction, rather than reinforcing its essential accuracy, implies that there might be a reason to question the relationship between reality and textual representation. Indeed, because of its complex and contradictory character, the war for O'Brien can never be faithfully rendered: "the only certainty," he writes, "is overwhelming ambiguity" (88). He goes on to say that "in a true war story nothing is ever absolutely true" (88). Yet it is through stories that experience is given the heft of truth: "the remembering is turned into a kind of rehappening" (36). And this "story-truth is truer sometimes than happening-truth" (203).

O'Brien is faced with a terrible paradox—a painful need to write the truth set against a realization that there is no unmediated access to truth. If for Michael Herr experience is mediated by language and culture, for O'Brien it is bound up with the process of memory and imagination. He can tell no truth that is not already contaminated by its imaginative reconstruction. To resolve this paradox, O'Brien emphasizes the process of story-making. For it is in this process that truth and falsehood, reality and representation, fact and fiction cohere. Paradoxically, it is by emphasizing artifice, by demonstrating the extent to which experience is an imaginative construct, that O'Brien attempts to identify the important truths buried within his memories of Vietnam. To O'Brien self-referentiality is a necessary feature of truthful writing, for only by emphasizing artifice can he write the truth, or as he suggests, "you tell lies to get at the truth" (quoted in Schroeder, 141).

To commercial critics, O'Brien's paradoxical mix of fact and fiction was an essential means of conveying the truth about Vietnam. Only one reviewer, Geoff Dyer in *New Statesman & Society*, seemed troubled by O'Brien's self-absorption. Dyer complains that through O'Brien's literary aesthetic, "what happened in Vietnam . . . gets enlarged and generalised into a concern with the nature and purpose of war stories." For Dyer, *The Things They Carried* can be boiled down to one central, trivial premise: "there is something remarkable . . . about making the transition from soldier to author." For other reviewers, *The Things They Carried* is remarkable in its ability to capture the essence of the war. Peter Prescott (in *Newsweek*) argues that the literary aesthetics used to describe previous wars are inappropriate for describing Vietnam. "Straightforward wars are built like novels," he writes, "they begin here, go to there, swell and subside along the way." But "Messy wars, like the one we fought in

Vietnam, lend themselves more readily to fragmented narratives." According to Robert Harris (in the *New York Times Book Review*), O'Brien "strives to get beyond literal descriptions" (since these are incapable of capturing the essence of the war) and to make "sense of the unreality of the war" by "distort[ing] that unreality even further in his fiction." Similarly, Michiko Kakutani (in the daily *New York Times*) praises O'Brien's ability to capture that war's hallucinatory mood, the oddly surreal atmosphere produced by jungle warfare, heavy drug use and the moral and political ambiguity of American involvement." To R. Z. Sheppard in *Time*, O'Brien succeeds "in conveying the free-fall sensation of fear and the surrealism of combat." And Julian Loose in the *Times Literary Supplement* explains that "By creating a work which so adroitly resists finality, O'Brien has been faithful to Vietnam and the stories told about it." For these reviewers, the war is a messy, unreal conflict that resists finality.

To describe the mass bombardment, defoliation, systematic assassinations, and planned destruction of the rural society of South Vietnam as "messy," however, is to domesticate it, to make it seem the result of bad management. It also views the war from an American perspective and profoundly trivializes the suffering of the Vietnamese. Nonetheless, this perception is an accurate assessment from the point of view of imperialists, for whom Vietnam was a "messy" war (as opposed to the "splendid, little war" the United States fought against Spain at the turn of the century or the alleged surgical precision of the Persian Gulf War) because it did not go as planned and, for a brief time, became something of an obstacle for American policy makers, a mess they have been trying to wash their hands of ever since.

To speak of the surreality and unreality of Vietnam is to mystify the war by confusing its perceptual experience with its material fact. True, from a soldier's viewpoint the chaos of battle was surreal, and some of the elements of this war—an unknown enemy; an alien landscape, culture, and climate; the vast difference between American military strength and the often underequipped Viet Cong; the jarring juxtaposition of American commercial culture and Vietnamese poverty—may have seemed "unreal." The problem with this perception is that it has dominated literary portrayals of the Vietnam War. To see Vietnam as resisting finality, as many critics have, is to see the war as inexplicable, therefore with no lesson to be learned. This denial of finality means denying any certain and explicit understanding of the war, as Kakutani makes clear when she speaks of "the moral and political ambiguities of American involvement"—a sentiment that mirrors exactly the liberal rewriting of the war, in which war crimes become moral and political ambiguities and an invasion becomes "involvement." (Likewise, Gary Krist in *Hudson Review* finds the soldiers in *The Things They Carried* "on their way to a . . . morally ambiguous goal" [692].) One need only transfer this interpretation to a context involving an enemy of the United States—the Soviet invasion of Afghanistan, for instance—to recognize the disguised politics embedded in Kakutani's seemingly apolitical evaluation. It is difficult to imagine a critic, in her evaluation of a novel about the Afghan war, asserting the moral and political ambiguities of Soviet involvement. (This comparison is somewhat misleading, since the justification for Soviet involvement in Afghanistan is more compelling than the justification for U.S. involvement in Vietnam.) In literary criticism, moral ambiguities are rarely politically ambiguous. That is, morality is seen as ambiguous, complex, and uncertain when it involves the United States, but when an official enemy's actions are scrutinized, no such nuanced, sensitive, and charitable interpretation is given. The harmful actions of enemies are always clearly immoral; the harmful actions of the United States are frequently clouded by ambiguities and complexities. (Kakutani herself faced no such moral ambiguity when writing about Rosalie Maggio's *The Bias-Free Word Finder*, condemning "the rigid orthodoxy" of "the self-appointed language police" and concocting predictably fanciful PC-speak, such as retitling *The Iceman Cometh* "The Ice Route Driver Cometh").

Reviews of *The Things They Carried* reveal a continuity running through the reception of Vietnam War literature, stretching back to *The Quiet American*. Walter Allen praised Greene for depicting "Human nature ... not [as] black and white but black and grey" (344), Irving Howe praised Kolpacoff for conceiving *The Prisoners of Quai Dong* "without any blatant propagandistic intent" (29), Roger Sales praised Herr for including in *Dispatches* "no politics, no certain morality, no clear outline of history" (35), and Kakutani praises O'Brien for his moral and political ambiguities. In each case, reviewers repudiate or transform whatever seems ideological, and they shower praise upon writers for creating narratives that are paradoxical, complex, ambiguous. However much the critical practice of reviewers may have changed since the 1950s, the ideology within commercial literary culture has remained much the same.

Academic critics have viewed *The Things They Carried* through a postmodern framework. This stress on the epistemological problematic of history has tended to occlude historical knowledge and to place emphasis upon literature for its own sake. For despite its pretensions to radical politics, postmodern literary criticism—at least as exemplified by the academic reception of *The Things They Carried*—seems little more than a new aestheticism, a belief in the power of storytelling and the literary imagination.

Continuing where reviewers left off, Steven Kaplan (first in an essay in *Critique*, later in a chapter of his *Understanding Tim O'Brien*) praises O'Brien for demonstrating the impossibility of understanding the war. "The only certain thing during the Vietnam War," Kaplan writes, "was that nothing was certain" (43). Similarly, he denies the possibility of finality, declaring that "events have no fixed or final meaning" (51). Consequently, no moral can be derived from the war, no lesson learned, since, in O'Brien's words, "a true war story is never moral" (76). To Kaplan, "The only thing that can be determined at the end of the story is its own indeterminacy" (47). Rather than question the appropriateness of O'Brien's textual playfulness and self-reference, Kaplan praises O'Brien for making readers "fully aware of being made a participant in a game, in a 'performative act'" (48), and he suggests that we can never fully know anything since all knowledge is language-dependent. It is not merely the war that is unknowable—everything is, since there can be no access to knowledge that is not mediated by language. For Kaplan, as for O'Brien, "events . . . deny the possibility of arriving at something called the 'full,' meaning certain and fixed 'truth'" (46). Full, certain, and fixed truth of course can never be achieved. No reputable philosopher or literary critic would assert such. More importantly, this denial of the full truth often seems to lead to a denial of any truth whatsoever. Thus all O'Brien can do, according to Kaplan, is "force . . . the reader to experience the impossibility of ever knowing what actually happened." Consequently,

> O'Brien liberates himself from the lonesome responsibility of remembering and trying to understand events. He also creates a community of individuals immersed in the act of experiencing the uncertainty of all events. . . . O'Brien saves himself by demonstrating in this book that the most important thing is to be able to recognize and accept that events have no fixed or final meaning and that the only meaning that events can have is one that emerges momentarily and then shifts and changes each time that the events come alive as they are remembered or portrayed. (Kaplan, 51)

Kaplan's argument points to the worst aspects of postmodern theory. At a time of American triumphalism, liberating oneself from the responsibility of remembering and understanding events is hardly emancipatory, since it is precisely this remembering and understanding that has been under assault. We do not need O'Brien to create a community immersed in the *uncertainty* of events—the mystifications and mythologies of American culture more than adequately reproduce this uncertainty. Kaplan's essay was published only two years after the Gulf War; yet he does not consider how effectively the Gulf War was sanitized and constructed as a noble mission. Against a background of overt propaganda, censorship, and jingoistic fervor, Kaplan argues for the vital importance of postmodern uncertainty. Such an argument, in its skepticism and acceptance of the status quo, is complicit in the erasure of historical memory and the reconstruction of the ideological system. What is needed is not a community immersed in the uncertainty of events but one that is educated in the details of capitalist exploitation and imperial enterprise.

Maria Bonn sympathizes with many of Kaplan's arguments. She argues that *The Things They Carried* "do[es] not teach" and suggests that if "O'Brien's readers have truly accepted his wily postmodern perceptions of the reader's relationship to the text then they know that they must reject any lessons" (14). Just as Kaplan finds O'Brien denying the possibility of finality, so Bonn declares that in *The Things They Carried* "any sense of conclusion or epiphany must be its own undoing" (14–15). Unlike Kaplan, however, she finds that O'Brien's "dizzying interplay of truth and fiction . . . is not solely aesthetic postmodern gamesmanship but a form that is a thematic continuation of the . . . concern throughout his career with the power and capability of story" (13).

More political than either Kaplan or Bonn, Philip Beidler in *Re-Writing America* sets out to demonstrate that Vietnam authors, continuing the spirit of the 1960s, are involved in a radical revision of American life and culture, an attempt "to reconstitute [American cultural] mythology as a medium both of historical self-reconsideration and, in the same moment, of historical self-renewal and even self-reinvention" (5). For Beidler, though, this struggle for historical self-renewal and reconsideration has little to do with history and much to do with these writers' formal strategies, since it is "through the bold embrace of new strategies of imaginative invention" that Vietnam authors "become in the fullest sense the creators of cultural myth for new times" (2).

Beidler does not consider the numerous and substantial obstacles that face any attempt to reconstitute cultural mythology. And he fails to recognize that his own argument relies on American cultural myth. Belief in the possibility of cultural and self-renewal and reinvention depends upon the myth of America as a land of opportunity, a nation in which anyone can reinvent him or herself and an entire culture can be rewritten through acts of the imagination. Beidler's reference to coming "new times" likewise repeats a familiar belief in the unrestrained promise of America. For Beidler, *The Things They Carried* helps reconstitute American cultural memory, a crucial task, he asserts, "in a country whose resolute belief in its historical exceptionalism, even after its involvement in a geopolitical tragedy like Vietnam, continues to be predicated on its easy capacity for historical amnesia" (28). The importance of *The Things They Carried* is to be found in its postmodern shattering of traditional categories of knowledge. Beidler explicitly connects such transgressions with cultural reinvention: *The Things They Carried* is a "rewriting of the old dialectic of facts and fictions and a literally exponential prediction of new contexts of vision and insight, of new worlds to remember, imagine, believe" (32–33); it is "the work of literature as personal sense making and cultural revision in the largest sense" (36). Despite his denunciation of American exceptionalism, Beidler premises his argument upon a similar belief—as is demonstrated by his reference to the new times, new contexts, and new worlds that may open up through *The Things They Carried*. In making this argument, Beidler ignores the immense institutional obstacles arrayed against real reinvention. He fails to define renewal and reinvention in any but the most general, abstract terms. He has no apparent political strategy or economic policy or ideology in mind, and his repeated mention of "self" suggests the individualist ethos that grounds his postmodern rhetoric.

Beidler also overlooks the considerable effort that has already gone into reconstructing the ideological system. Ignoring this background, he views Vietnam War literature as a significant force for cultural reinvention, for rewriting America. He does not consider the possibility that this literature—and the culture that shapes, produces, distributes, and receives it—may, because of institutional constraints, be involved in a conservative rather than a progressive reinvention. As this book argues, literature and literary culture have indeed been rewriting America, but it has been a rewriting that obscures a radical, materialist critique and places in its stead an individualist, ethnocentric, and ahistorical appreciation of ambiguity and fragmentation.

The blurring of distinctions between fact and fiction is not, as Beidler and others suggest, an inherently radical gesture. This misperception stems from a postmodern reading of hierarchies and categories as by definition authoritarian. By transgressing borders and bringing into question the whole notion of categorization, or so the argument goes, O'Brien is involved in a radical project. Yet American culture hardly needs O'Brien, or academic postmodernists for that matter, to deconstruct fact and fiction. With its quasi-historical popular entertainments, its fictionalizations and historical reenactments and sensationalist news, American popular culture is deeply involved in problematizing the fact/fiction distinction.

Beidler's argument that O'Brien's achievement is "cultural revision in the *largest sense*" is reminiscent of Frances Kunkel's assertion that we "*enlarge our perspectives* by abandoning Greene's views of American foreign policy" (150, emphasis added). Beidler's "largest sense" really amounts to a narrowing of perspective, since in his discussion of *The Things They Carried* there is virtually no mention of actual history. The reinvention of our categories of fact and fiction is in effect an erasure of fact and a preoccupation with fiction, with aesthetics, with the literary imagination. Beidler never refers to the countryside devastated by American weapons or the society shattered by American military policy or the people who fought against and suffered because of the Americans. Instead, he writes that "Vietnam must remain . . . out there somewhere between memory and imagining" (35), out there in the realm of pure artifice.

Like Beidler, Donald Ringnalda in *Fighting and Writing the Vietnam War* singles out O'Brien's blurring of the fact and fiction distinction. He argues that in his work O'Brien has increasingly demonstrated the arbitrariness of this distinction, moving from "a solid line to a dotted line to one that sometimes disappears altogether" (103), finally "spurn[ing] the Western paradigm of Manichaean dualism, which convinces most of the people most of the time that they can tell the difference between reality and fiction" (104). As his allusion to P. T. Barnum ("you can fool most of the people most of the time") implies, Ringnalda believes the distinction between fact and fiction to be little more than a carny trick. For Ringnalda, seeing through this con and deconstructing the fact/fiction split is an act of vital *political* importance because it is precisely the inability to do so that initiated U.S. involvement in Vietnam: "This genre sureness got us into Vietnam in the first place." Ringnalda's argument goes something like this: unable to acknowledge "the powerful influence of our positivist paradigm," America did not recognize that its belief system—what it perceived as fact, in particular "its righteous anti-Communist paradigm" (101)—was fiction. If the United States had had a more postmodern sensibility, it would not have been presumptuous enough to believe it could organize the world into good and evil, communist and capitalist, and would not have attempted to impose its "epistemologically crude and naive" (102) view of reality upon Vietnam.

There are several problems with this analysis. For one thing, if we truly are unable to distinguish between fact and fiction, on what grounds is Ringnalda's postmodernism to be privileged over realism? Underlying his argument, after all, is the notion that postmodernism is in some sense a more accurate (because less reductive and more complex) way to view the world. *The Things They Carried* is said to be a better book than John Del Vecchio's realist novel *The 13th Valley* because O'Brien's uncertainty about the distinction between fact and fiction is truer to the facts of Vietnam than Del Vecchio's positivism. "To offer up a hallucinatory experience as straight history, as an accumulation of facts and information" the way Del Vecchio does, is, according to Ringnalda, "to mediate that experience out of existence"; it is to use "a language disconnected from the reality it purports to express" (16). But the question persists: how can Ringnalda posit a knowable, quantifiable reality if it is impossible to tell the difference between fact and fiction? On what basis can Del Vecchio's facts and information and language be disconnected from reality and O'Brien's uncertainty essential to it? Ringnalda would argue that the reality of Vietnam was chaotic and that a positivist epistemology, with its notion that experience is clear and verifiable, cannot possibly hope to convey this chaos—only a postmodern epistemology captures something of this experience.

Ringnalda sees the choice as between postmodernism and positivism; thus he establishes his position as the only alternative to an admittedly crude and naive epistemology. He sets up a straw epistemology that is easily knocked down. The problem with this opposition between postmodernism and positivism can be seen in Ringnalda's choice of metaphors. He argues that "Sense-making narratives of realism continue to display the will to superimpose the clarity of [Norman] Rockwell over the ambiguity of Dali in our Vietnam experience" (6). For Ringnalda, realism equals Rockwell, postmodernism Dali. Of course, realism does not have to be reduced to the nostalgic fantasies of Rockwell. But Ringnalda's argument would be far less convincing if he were comparing the surrealism of Dali to the realism of a Breughel or a Goya. In seeing the choice as between postmodernism and positivism, Ringnalda seems unaware of recent work in the philosophy of science by the likes of Richard Boyd, Roy Bhaskar, and Hilary Putnam that offers a much more sophisticated realist epistemology. As Gregory Meyerson explains:

> Recent theories of sophisticated realism have . . . seriously under-mined the assumptions enabling deconstructive criticism. First, realism need not be an epistemological absolutism. As a result, reasons and evidence need not be ultimate, need not be "an absolute guarantee." . . . In recent realist discussions of theory confirmation, evidence forms part of a larger chain-of-reasoning argument. Evidence itself is in a broad sense theory dependent; theoretical considerations can, in turn, be evidential. Both points undermine the theory/observation distinction and a foundationalist reading of the distinction between direct and indirect evidence that follows in its wake. (58)

Ringnalda goes on to suggest that America was unable to perceive how positivism/realism distorted its beliefs because of its "fear of disorder and complexity, and . . . addiction to the righteous power over that disorder and complexity." To Ringnalda, this "cultural imperative against disorder" (25) explains the American war in Vietnam. Realism is an inappropriate literary strategy, therefore, not merely because it is unfaithful to the complexity of the war but because it attempts to impose order on chaos. For Ringnalda, the connection between Del Vecchio's realism and "simplifying a disorderly landscape with agent orange is more than metaphorical: it stems from the same culturally induced urge: to render chaos into simplified order" (26). Realism, on Ringnalda's account, *is* imperialism.

The corollary to this argument is true for Ringnalda as well. If U.S. policy is based on positivist premises and a need to impose order, then Viet Cong policy must be based on postmodernist premises and an acceptance of chaos. Ringnalda sees Vietnam quite explicitly as a war between American realism and Viet Cong postmodernism: "the paradigm we carried with us to Vietnam was that of the 'omnisciently narrated' corporation, which functions with hierarchical, vertical management.... By contrast, the Vietcong were organized more in terms of postmodern literature.... In other words, the Vietcong cadres were not dependent parts of the whole, they were inextricable, interdependent manifestations of the whole. The organizational principle, more lateral than vertical, was based more on patterns of surprise and unpredictability than on structures of power and domination" (11). Ringnalda goes on to argue that the vast majority of Vietnam War novels mistakenly adopt a realistic aesthetic that "emulate[s] the narrow conventional preoccupations and presumptions of America's military leaders in Vietnam. They refuse to relinquish the traditional 'firepower' of authorial, 'managerial' control" (12). Specifically, Ringnalda identifies four ways that "most Vietnam novels mirror the military operations": "They are enamored of the sense-making 'power' of maps (literal and figurative); they limit themselves to linear time; they overestimate the capabilities of technology; and finally, they are mired in cultural narcissism that results in racism and a shocking ignorance of Vietnam and its people" (13). For someone honestly concerned with cultural narcissism and racism, Ringnalda seems unaware of the extent to which his own argument depends upon cultural essentialism in its suggestion that the Viet Cong "used the strength of our technology the way Eastern martial arts absorb and redirect an opponent's aggression, strength, and momentum" (9) and that "the East has always had a much different understanding of chaos" (29). Even if we ignore this essentialism (and the inappropriateness of reading a revolutionary war against U.S. imperialism through first world literary/cultural conceits), it is worth noting that Ringnalda's argument works just as well the other way around: American policy can be associated with postmodernism and Viet Cong policy with realism. The advanced weaponry used by American troops produced, it could be argued, a Baudrillardian hyperreality for pilots and anyone else witnessing this destruction from afar. For the victims of these weapons, however, the war was all too real. It is hard to read the following remembrance, by The Ngoc Phan, as in any way postmodern:

> The houses had been bombed many times before, but that time we were hit by napalm. We called it the Battle of Pouring Fire. We

had been living in tunnels with only the clothes on our back. And
when they told us we had to go to an evacuation center we came
out, and that's when they dropped the napalm. We were all burned.
At first we couldn't find Kim Phuc [The Ngoc Phan's nine-year-old
daughter]. We buried the two children and went to look for her.
Three days later we found her at the hospital in Ho Chi Minh City.
They had put her with the dead bodies, and later saw she was still
breathing. She looked like she was dead, with all her flesh burned
off. She cried all the time, it was so painful. From 1972 until 1984
her skin continued to burn, twelve years. (quoted in Hess, 109)

Likewise, American soldiers' cultural confusion and perpetual awareness of
difference and their ability to move rapidly from one place to another can be
read as postmodern, whereas the Viet Cong's respect for Vietnamese tradition, its attempts to preserve village solidarity, its closeness to nature, and its
relative lack of technology can be read in terms of realism.

In defining postmodernism many critics distinguish between an earlier
era of monopoly capitalism and a contemporary world of late capitalism, whose
features consist of, in Fredric Jameson's words, "a new international division of
labor, a vertiginous new dynamic in international banking ... the flight of
production to advanced Third World areas, along with all the more familiar social consequences" (xix). To these critics postmodernism is associated
with—is, according to Jameson, the cultural logic of—late capitalism. Since
the United States fought to keep Vietnam from withdrawing from the global
capitalist system (and from thereby serving as a model for other states intent
on doing so—in other words, to maintain Vietnam as a site to be exploited by
transnational corporations within the era of late capitalism), it is odd, to say
the least, to associate the Viet Cong with postmodernism, to view their third-
world nationalism and anti-capitalism as the embodiment of a first world,
capitalist conceit. But as Philip Melling explains, "What the American experience reveals, says the postmodernist, is a level of sophistication and enterprise
that is far more intriguing and relevant to the world in which we live than the
primitive ideology of an aspiring third world country" (119).

For others, postmodernism is also frequently defined by its opposition to
what Jean-François Lyotard labels "master narratives"—any central, ordering,
legitimizing narrative, such as Marxism. The Viet Cong, of course, was a revolutionary people's army. Its politics were explicitly Marxist. By associating it
with a literary/cultural theory that denies the validity of Marxism (and that
grew out of Lyotard's and others' post-1968 anticommunism), Ringnalda in
effect erases the defining ideology of the Viet Cong for the sake of superficial
similarities between VC organization and postmodern theory.

Predictably, Ringnalda associates realism with a "cultural narcissism that results in racism and a shocking ignorance of Vietnam and its people" (13). In so doing, he repeats the familiar idea that postmodernism provides space for individuals, groups, and beliefs that have been marginalized by the various metanarratives that make up the Western tradition. Yet it is precisely the postmodern elements of *The Things They Carried* that contribute to its solipsism and ethnocentrism. In attempting to challenge the concept of an autonomous subject, O'Brien writes a text that is obsessed with self; he details the uncertain effects of an unreal war upon an unknowable self but fails to examine its all too real effects upon the Vietnamese. This oversight echoes American culture's repeated excision of Vietnamese suffering from the historical record. Even on "the rare occasions when the devastating consequences of the war are noted," write Herman and Chomsky, "care is taken to sanitize the reports so as to eliminate the U.S. role" (83). Part of this role, between 1965 and 1967, was to unleash 4.5 million tons of aerial bombardment upon Indochina—about nine times the tonnage dropped in the Pacific during World War II (including Hiroshima and Nagasaki). By the end of the war the United States had dropped seven million tons of bombs on Vietnam—more than twice the tonnage dropped on Europe and Asia during the second world war, or almost one 500-pound bomb for every Vietnamese (Zinn 469). While many Americans can give a rough estimate of U.S. casualties, they consistently underestimate Vietnamese casualties. According to public opinion polls circa 1990, Americans on average estimated 100,000 Vietnamese deaths, missing the true figure by only two million (Chomsky, *World Orders*, 96). Such ignorance of the lethal consequences of U.S. militarism is due to a process of historical revision that has been ongoing since the end of the war.

The logic behind the repeated association of postmodernism with the Vietnam War is explained by Kate Beaird Meyers. "Because Vietnam is so different from other wars in modern memory," Meyers writes, "no good model exists for translating it into a traditional chronological historical narrative" (547). She argues that the war presents many problems for historians: there was no specific starting date, official facts conflict with observable phenomena, and the Vietnam war was something new—a war of images. And most significant of all—"the American public was never told why Americans were dying in Vietnam." Because it has "blast[ed] into fragments any ideas we might have had about the way wars are supposed to be," Meyers asserts, "the Vietnam War may be the perfect subject for postmodern history" (549). Just as critics agree with O'Brien's deconstruction of the fact/fiction split, seeing it as a necessary dismantling of an unjustifiable distinction, so Meyers argues that "'factual history,' which is based on the 'fiction' of language, cannot exist" (550). If Meyers can find no specific starting date for the war, Milton

Bates can find no specific end date: "Was it over in 1973," he asks, "when the last American troops were withdrawn from Vietnam? In 1975, when South Vietnam fell to the North? In 1991 when President Bush declared the United States had 'kicked the Vietnam Syndrome once and for all' with its victory in the Persian Gulf? In 1995, when President Clinton extended full diplomatic recognition to the government in Hanoi? Or will the war last as long as there are people whose lives have been affected by it?" (253).

Postmodern consensus about the inability to distinguish between fact and fiction and the inherent falsehood of any organizing metanarrative has already had the effect of excluding radical critique—or for that matter any coherent explanation of the war—from most discussions of Vietnam War literature. And it has led to a championing of literary texts that similarly avoid explanation. Thus in *Dispatches* Herr writes:

> You couldn't find two people who agreed about when [the war] began. . . . Mission intellectuals like 1954 as the reference date; if you saw as far back as World War II and the Japanese occupation you were practically a historical visionary. "Realists" said that it began for us in 1961, and the common run of Mission flack insisted on 1965, post-Tonkin Resolution, as though all the killing that had gone before wasn't really war. Anyway, you couldn't use standard methods to date the doom; might as well say that Vietnam was where the Trail of Tears was headed all along, the turnaround point where it would touch and come back to form a containing perimeter; might just as well lay it on the proto-Gringos who found the New England woods too raw and empty for their peace and filled them up with their own imported devils. (51)

Similarly, in *Going After Cacciato* O'Brien speaks of an ideological uncertainty:

> He didn't know who was right, or what was right; he didn't know if it was a war of self-determination or self-destruction, outright aggression or national liberation; he didn't know which speeches to believe, which books, which politicians; he didn't know if nations would topple like dominoes or stand separate like trees; he didn't know who really started the war, or why, or when, or with what motives; he didn't know if it mattered; he saw sense in both sides of the debate, but he did not know where truth lay; he didn't know if Communist tyranny would prove worse in the long run than the tyrannies of Ky or Thieu or Khanh—he simply didn't know. And who did? Who really did? (313)

Thirteen years later in *The Things They Carried* O'Brien has come no closer to understanding the war. He repeats this earlier uncertainty with a series of rhetorical questions: "Was it a civil war? A war of national liberation or simple aggression? Who started it, and when, and why? What really happened to the USS *Maddox* on that dark night in the Gulf of Tonkin? Was Ho Chi Minh a Communist stooge, or a nationalist savior, or both, or neither? What about the Geneva Accords? What about SEATO and the Cold War? What about dominoes?" (44).

As a consequence of the postmodern epistemology and aesthetic that have come to dominate literary representations of the war, Herr cannot tell whether 1954, the year in which the French were defeated at Dien Bien Phu and in which President Eisenhower pledged U.S. support for Diem, or the forced migration of the Cherokee in 1838 is a more likely date for the beginning of the Vietnam War. From a Marxist perspective, there is a continuity between these events, since both resulted from colonialist expansion, from the need to acquire and control territory and increase national power. But Herr's and O'Brien's cataloguing of interpretations and questions is meant to suggest the unfathomable complexity and moral ambiguity that define Vietnam, not to detail the historical continuities of American imperialism. Such complexity mirrors postmodernists' contention that no explanation has a privileged connection to the truth. And it is reminiscent of literary culture's traditional sense that the world is far too rich and ambiguous to be reduced to a simple political lesson. To O'Brien's set of questions and to the general feeling that Vietnam is unreal and inexplicable, we could append another set posed by Michael Parenti: "Why has the U.S. government never supported social revolutionary forces against right-wing governments? Could it possibly do so? If not, why not? Why in the post-war era has the U.S. overthrown a dozen or more popularly elected left-reformist democracies? Why has it fostered close relations with just about all the right-wing autocracies on earth?" (*Sword and the Dollar*, 191). The most logical and coherent explanation for this history is that in its foreign policy the United States has placed the interests of capital above almost all other concerns. While some of the questions O'Brien and others ask may be difficult to answer with absolute certitude, any general understanding of the Vietnam War should start with recognition of America's consistent support for right-wing regimes and its opposition to left-reformist democracies in order to, in Parenti's words, "mak[e] the world safe for ... plutocracy" (*Sword and the Dollar*, 191). Yet in these catalogues of questions and indeterminacies no one points to the kind of argument offered by Parenti, not even as one out of many possible interpretations. While literary critics may agree that all explanations have potentially the same connection to truth, they almost invariably exclude from consideration Marxist theories of imperialism. In seeking to understand why Kiowa died, O'Brien writes, "when a man died, there had to be blame. . . . You could blame the war. You could blame the idiots who made the war. You could blame Kiowa for going to it. . . . You could blame the enemy. You could blame the mortar rounds. You could blame people who were too lazy to read a newspaper, who were bored by the daily body counts, who switched channels at the mention of politics. You could blame whole nations. You could blame God. You could blame the munitions makers or Karl Marx or a trick of fate or an old man in Omaha who forgot to vote" (198–199). The only certain cause of Kiowa's death, according to O'Brien, is its direct cause: "In the field . . . the causes were immediate. A moment of carelessness or bad judgment or plain stupidity" (199). Yet some causes are more proximate and explanatory than others. Robert McNamara is more responsible for deaths in Vietnam than an old man in Omaha who forgets to vote. The board of directors of Dow Chemical are more blameworthy than people who switched channels at the mention of politics. The people who made the war and the munitions makers (both of whom, unlike Karl Marx and, earlier, Ho Chi Minh, O'Brien refuses to name) deserve the blame.

Besides ignoring the ideological complicity of the postmodern refusal to distinguish between fact and fiction, between true and false histories, contemporary literary critics, in their repeated endorsement of a postmodern rendering of the war, have failed to recognize that postmodernism itself arose during and has taken part in the reactionary rewriting of the war and repudiation of left radicalism. As Alex Callinicos explains:

> The political odyssey of the 1968 generation is . . . crucial to the widespread acceptance of the idea of a postmodern epoch in the 1980s. This was the decade when those radicalized in the 1960s and early 1970s began to enter middle age. Usually they did so with all hope of socialist revolution gone—indeed, often having ceased to . . . believe in the desirability of any such revolution. Most of them had by then come to occupy some sort of professional, managerial or administrative position, to have become members of the new middle class, at a time when the overconsumptionist dynamic of Western capitalism offered this class rising living standards. . . . This conjuncture—the prosperity of the Western new middle class combined with the political disillusionment of many of its most articulate members—provides the context to the proliferating talk of postmodernism. (168)

As upwardly mobile professionals entering managerial positions (or as those who seek to do so), many contemporary academic literary critics are sympathetic to postmodernism because it gives their scholarship a radical edge at no cost, and sometimes even at benefit, to their careers. For those who write of O'Brien's deconstruction of fact and fiction, who associate the Viet Cong with chaos and the Americans with a rage for order, who refuse to impose any form of coherent narrative on the Vietnam War, little they write is significantly at odds with dominant belief. Their critique might be more complex and even more progressive than that of establishment policy makers, but it rarely confronts the issue of class exploitation/imperialism and its connection to the war.

The reception of *The Things They Carried*, therefore, suggests that even into the 1990s, dominant modes of literary analysis are frequently used to avoid serious ideological and materialist critique, while seeming to do the opposite. Criticism that has countered such prevailing views in order to read Vietnam War literature for what it reveals about U.S. imperialism and capitalist hegemony is atypical of both traditional and contemporary critical practice, within and without the academy; it appeared only after the tumult of the 1960s and the horrors of the war; and it is now under steady assault, rhetorically and financially, from the forces of capital.

Note

1. The blurbs cited on the Penguin paperback give a good idea of the kind of hyperbole that greeted *The Things They Carried*. "As good as any piece of literature can get" (*Chicago Sun-Times*), "one of the most persuasive works of any kind to arise out of any war" (*Hartford Courant*), "a matchless literary book" (*Kansas City Star*), "writing so powerful that it steals your breath" (*Milwaukee Journal*), *The Things They Carried* "joins the work of Crane and Hemingway and Mailer as great war literature" (*Tampa Tribune & Times*), and Tim O'Brien is "the best American writer of his generation" (*San Francisco Examiner*).

CARL S. HORNER

Challenging the Law of Courage and Heroic Identification in Tim O'Brien's If I Die in a Combat Zone and The Things They Carried

In his autobiographic text, *If I Die in a Combat Zone: Box Me up and Ship Me Home*, and in his novel, *The Things They Carried*, Tim O'Brien questions the presumed sanctity of the oldest male law. Courage and masculinity, so-called "professionalism," the "old order" (*If I Die* 192), grace under pressure, or the collective male psyche could, O'Brien writes, blind a man into stupidity during the Vietnam War. Not that he could always rely on published information or even rationally determine a wise course in the call of duty, but a citizen had the obligation to discover whether business leaders, politicians, and military officers had moral, legal, and therefore truly evident causes for sanctioning violence in Vietnam. Blind or obsessive duty for the sake of honor, God, and country might be bravery to a fault, or nothing more than "manliness, crudely idealized" (*If I Die* 142).

Courage is only one part of virtue, O'Brien explains, alluding to the warnings of Plato. Courage cannot be separated from wisdom, temperance, and justice. Once a man sheds heroic identification and merit deeds; once he refuses either to compromise his morality, to kill illegally, or to entrap himself in the futile sacrifice of "a war fought for uncertain reasons" (*If I Die* 135); once he seeks inwardly and deliberately for the meaning of courage (an obligation more frightening and dangerous than prescriptive duty), he escapes mechanical bravery and the spiritual death that blind conscription

From *War, Literature, and the Arts* 11, no. 1 (Spring–Summer 1999): 256–67. © 1999 by Carl S. Horner.

can produce. That is, the soldier who responds not to what he really believes but to the expectations of indoctrinated parents, small-town neighbors, sergeants, and lieutenants is charged, O'Brien writes, with the passion, the ignorance "merely" of "a well-disguised cowardice" (*If I Die* 135).

Throughout gender history, men have been pressured to react to deadly crisis according to the sacred rules of a male honor code. From Odysseus to King Arthur, from Ulysses to George Washington, and from Aeneas to Norman Schwarzkopf, clearly the most widely accepted values of integrity, dignity, respect, self-respect, valor, and thus unquestioned masculinity hinge upon a commissioned response to fear and duty. Rational control over the emotion of fear or doubt; strength not only of body but also of mind—the tangential strength, that is, of the gifted athlete and military wizard; appropriate aggression fed by a competitive spirit; full-pitch confidence to win against overwhelming odds; and utter loyalty to duty, to God, to country, to family, and to friends collectively define the classic male hero. Here is the meaning of inventiveness, resilience, and endurance in the male universe. Here is the legendary crisis crusher, the icon of national and international glory and fame, the Captain, my Captain of moral common sense and duty, the human bush hog cutting the memorial path to higher truth. "It's the old story," Major Callicles insists in *If I Die in a Combat Zone*. "Guts to stand up for what's right. . . . It's not standing around passively hoping for things to happen right; it's going out and being tough and sharp-thinkin' and *making* things happen right" (194–195). Clearly, undaunted courage lies at the heart of this "crucible of men" and epic "events" (22–23).

A "blond, meticulously fair, brave, tall, [and] blue-eyed" Captain Johanson would be recognized traditionally and yet blindly as his "nation's pride" for his classic masculinity when in "the steady, blood-headed intensity of Sir Lancelot" (*If I Die* 131, 144) he charges across a rice paddy to kill a Vietcong soldier nearly at point-blank range. Did he act for the benefit or the safety of his platoon? Was his deed an act of self-sacrifice? Was this an "ag-ile, mo-bile, and hos-tile" man "resigned to bullets and brawn" (*If I Die* 44, 91)? Or was this mission nothing more than an adrenaline rush—not bravery, not courage really, but mindless aggression? "It's the charge, the light brigade with only one man" sailing neither with fear nor with regret into harm's way, O'Brien cautions, that typically comes to mind "first" in the classification of heroes. Men who charge the enemy despite their fear of death "are remembered as brave, win or lose." Here are the sacred heroes forever tall, true, and tough—forever rough, ready, and rugged—and men like Johanson confess that they would "rather be brave" in this way "than almost anything" else in life. These men are truly "heroes forever" in war history and in literature, but we must not conclude that "courage" presupposes the bloody "charge" (*If I Die* 131).

"Courage is nothing to laugh at, not if it is proper courage and exercised by men who know what they do is proper" (133), O'Brien writes in *If I Die in a Combat Zone*, arguing that if we are not thinking, we are not human. If we are not thinking, by extension we are not brave in the human dimension. "Proper courage is wise courage," O'Brien explains, alluding to Plato's dialectic of noble bravery in "Laches." "It's acting wisely, acting wisely when fear would have a man act otherwise. It is the endurance of the soul in spite of fear—wisely" (133).

Mindless charge has its place in war—indeed, force can generate the power necessary to win a deadly conflict. But we must not confuse crude aggression with the noble cause enlivened by courage. Doing the best that any individual can do, according to his own conscience, keeps common sense and meaning in the acts of courage. Routine physical acts, the thing to do at the time, raw valor, doing what everyone else is doing to avoid shame, acting bravely "out of a spirit of righteousness . . . necessity . . . resignation" (*If I Die* 45), merely following orders—is that acting gallantly? What might be classified or even decorated with the Congressional Medal of Honor as courageous mentality could like the "endless march" of duty honestly be reduced to a physical response to stressful experience with "no volition, no will, because it was automatic, it was anatomy . . . a kind of inertia, a kind of emptiness, a dullness of desire and intellect and conscience and hope and human sensibility" (*Things* 15).

Human courage comes not from the hypothalamus, not from the anterior pituitary or adrenal glands, and not from any other direct or indirect influence on a fight-or-flight response to stress, including the central nervous system and the testicles, but from the clear thinking cortex of the brain. "Men must *know* what they do is courageous," O'Brien argues in *If I Die in a Combat Zone*—that is, "they must *know* it is right, and that kind of knowledge is wisdom and nothing else" (137). Be it Plato's rationalism or Heidegger's and Sartre's existentialism, acting knowingly and thoughtfully is the human condition.

Within this self-limiting vision of courage, O'Brien hesitates to celebrate many brave men. "Either they are stupid and do not know what is right," including one Alpha Company soldier who had no thoughts about his participation in the war—certainly, no high thoughts about morality or politics—and who only wanted to get out of Vietnam alive. "Or they know what is right and cannot bring themselves to do it. Or they know what is right and do it, but do not feel and understand the fear that must be overcome" (*If I Die* 137). Holding ground on principle, or for no other reason than to hold it, as in the example of a cow taking countless rounds from O'Brien's company in a free-fire zone, is neither courage nor endurance. It is mortal stupidity.

Of course, O'Brien is not the first writer to challenge the law of courage, warning that mindless assault, even for honorable causes, loses the human dimension of bravery. Although Hemingway vehemently opposed the psychoanalytic view popular in his day that each individual suffers a point at which his mind or body will break down under pressure, Colonel Lum Edwards explained that even during the most frightening combat of the 1944 Hurtgen campaign Hemingway was never "impressed by reckless bravado." While he "admired the man who could see clearly what was necessary to do and had the courage to do it, regardless of the percentage of risk involved," never did Hemingway identify "raw courage," or suicidal aggression, as honorable or even as desirable "unless it was the only way of getting the job done." Impressed by Hemingway's love of direct action over diction, Edwards concluded that his friend practiced his honor code sincerely each of his eighteen days in Hurtgenwald:

> I never saw him act foolishly in combat. He understood war and man's part in it to a better degree than most people ever will. He had an excellent sense of the situation. While wanting to contribute, he knew very well when to proceed and when it was best to wait awhile. (qtd. in Baker 435)

Despite the attractive filter that Hemingway placed on courage—essentially, that a life-threatening event in war (or in any deadly crisis) is merely a test, a test not only of courage and endurance but also of dignity—O'Brien notes in *If I Die in a Combat Zone* that simple stoicism is not a consistently adequate measure of bravery under any circumstance in war:

> It's too easy to affect grace, and it's too hard to see through it. . . . Grace under pressure means you can confront things gracefully or squeeze out of them gracefully. But to make those two things equal with the easy word "grace" is wrong. Grace under pressure is not courage. (142–143)

If Hemingway had lived under the daily grind of a combat soldier for a year or more, rather than drifting in and out of deadly conflict as a correspondent, the law of averages would have shattered his stoicism and thus his own law of courage, as the ironies, uncertainties, and cruelties of the war theater would contradict any man's inflexible belief.

Shoved or hit in his childhood schoolyard, any man of Alpha Company would fight. Rather than lose dignity or the appearance of courage, he would scream and snarl and flail the air and flail his enemies in the cruel power and glory of male potency. Indeed, public confessions about the fear of death were more than "bad luck" or "the ultimate self-fulfilling prophecy," all of which was strictly "taboo" (*If I Die* 138) for any soldier in any combat platoon during the Vietnam War. The collective male honor code precludes the contemplation of fear. Admitting fear is simply illegal or shameful in the male universe. The men of Alpha Company were nurtured in the same laws of masculinity as any other soldier in any other war. A man must not cry. He must not whine or complain. Worse, he must not lose control over his emotions or run in the heat of crisis. He must at least wear the mask of bravery in all conflict. The burden of fear and the shame that he would have to suffer if he let it creep into his face haunted even the toughest soldier of Alpha Company. Everyone "carried the common secret of cowardice barely restrained, the instinct to run or freeze or hide." Certainly, under the crushing weight of stress, violence, and ordnance, the male role "was the heaviest burden of all, for it could never be put down." Carrying "the soldier's greatest fear," the terror not of death but "the fear of blushing," the men of Alpha Company "were too frightened to be cowards." No high "dreams of glory or honor" threatened their dignity, merely "the blush of dishonor." They might even sneer at death in order not to be embarrassed by it. Indeed, men "died so as not to die of embarrassment" (*Things* 20–21). Here we see to what extent soldiers are driven in war, the bright center stage of the collective male psyche, not only by the Darwinism of androgen, testosterone, and adrenaline that inflames their aggressive spirits but also by the far more imperial grip of social Darwinism.

The "secret" to success in all crises, Bill brags to Jake in Hemingway's *The Sun Also Rises*, is "never be daunted." Of course, we can presume that Bill has been frightened by the violent experiences that any boy or man must endure in social reality, but he must always be politically correct, and thus he will not show his fear. "Not in public. If I begin to feel daunted I'll go off by myself" (73). The silly Lion believes that he will be king over the forests of Oz if he develops not heart and not mind but courage. Ironically, Juno fails to realize in Virgil's *Aeneid* that men value courage over life and safety; thus, her effort to save Turnus from certain death in fated battle with Aeneas only frustrates the man beyond either the fear or the pain of death. "The horror of it!" Turnus shrieks, realizing that he has fled the battlefield in pursuit not of his rival but only of an apparition of Aeneas. Here for the classic soldier is "a fault so grave," a "disgrace" and "shame" so unforgivable and "terrible" (271–272), that only Juno can restrain her mortal from instantly killing himself on his own sword or foolishly attempting to swim back to land in order to regain his dignity in the heat of war.

In order to protect themselves from shame and forbidden fear, some soldiers in Alpha Company "carried themselves with a sort of wistful resignation."

Other soldiers wore the masks of "pride or stiff soldierly discipline or good human or macho zeal." All of them were inwardly "afraid of dying," the bravest leaders like Captain Johanson and the toughest grunts like Rat Kiley, "but they were even more afraid to show it" (*Things* 19).

"All of us, I suppose, like to believe that in a moral emergency we will behave like the heroes of our youth," O'Brien writes—that is, "bravely and forthrightly, without thought of personal loss or discredit." Alan Ladd and Humphrey Bogart had impressed O'Brien's childhood dreams in the formidable way in which a hero responds to crisis. In his impressionable childhood, O'Brien incubated the belief that he "would simply tap a secret reservoir" of his "moral capital" (*Things* 43) and conquer mounting evil as if he were the new generation's Frederick Henry, Captain Vere, or Shane (*If I Die* 139). However, the "old image" of himself "as a man of conscience and courage" (*Things* 60) collided with the Darwinian forces of the Vietnam War. Would his decision to go either to Canada where he could live according to his conscience or to Vietnam where he would answer his call to duty despite his conscience result in an honest act of courage? If he did succumb to national pride, would he find the path to truth and honor promised by his culture or merely kill the citizen's obligation to follow his inner voices in matters of political dispute?

Despite respected warnings from Ezra Pound that soldiers have entrapped themselves in war "from fear of weakness" or "from fear of censure" (qtd. in O'Brien, *If I Die* 37), or from fear of not being manly, and despite O'Brien's research into the political contradictions of Ho Chi Minh, the Gulf of Tonkin, the Geneva Accords, SEATO, and the division, if not the "moral confusion," among "smart" American politicians who "could not agree on even the most fundamental matters of public policy," O'Brien suffered the gnawing pressure to abandon his belief "that you don't make war without knowing why" (*Things* 44). This "moral split," he explains, caused him to experience "a kind of schizophrenia" (*Things* 48), even to the degree of hallucinating the faces and voices of his parents, his hometown friends, alien neighbors and civic leaders, Civil and World War veterans, high school cheerleaders, his best friend who died in her childhood, a memory of his cowboy hat and mask, Jane Fonda, Gary Cooper, and a myriad of other polar impressions. Although the events "On the Rainy River" are invented in *The Things They Carried* only to evoke O'Brien's confusion and anguish that he more autobiographically expresses in *If I Die in a Combat Zone*, the feeling of psychic warfare draws us into a haunting truth:

> I couldn't make up my mind. I feared the war, yes, but I also feared exile. I was afraid of walking away from my own life, my friends

and my family, my whole history, everything that mattered to me. I feared losing the respect of my parents. I feared the law. I feared ridicule and censure. (*Things* 48)

Cleanth Brooks writes that moral pressure is exerted as "the essential ether" (52) in American small towns. Indeed, aliens to community codes risk the deadly loneliness not only of spoken and unspoken ridicule but also of self-doubt. Besides his mother and father, whose hurt over a son's resolution to go against the stream he could vividly imagine, O'Brien could picture the emotional violence of town leaders and gossips if they were to discuss his decision to follow his conscience:

> My hometown was a conservative little spot on the prairie, a place where tradition counted, and it was easy to imagine people sitting around a table down at the old Gobbler Café on Main Street, coffee cups poised, the conversation slowly zeroing in on the young O'Brien kid, how the damned sissy had taken off for Canada. At night, when I couldn't sleep, I'd sometimes carry on fierce arguments with those people. I'd be screaming at them, telling them how much I detested their blind, thoughtless, automatic acquiescence to it all, their simple-minded patriotism, their prideful ignorance, their love-it-or-leave-it platitudes, how they were sending me off to fight a war they didn't understand and didn't want to understand. I held them responsible. By God, yes, I *did*. All of them—I held them personally and individually responsible—the polyestered Kiwanis boys, the merchants and farmers, the pious churchgoers, the chatty housewives, the PTA and the Lions club and the Veterans of Foreign Wars and the fine upstanding gentry out at the country club. They didn't know Bao Dai from the man in the moon. They didn't know history. They didn't know the first thing about Diem's tyranny, or the nature of Vietnamese nationalism, or the long colonialism of the French. (*Things* 48–49)

Of course, O'Brien could not discuss his inner turmoil with anyone so heavily locked into conservative beliefs about men, heroes, and war. And even though he recognized the irony of giving up honest feelings about himself in order to live a life without conflict with people whom he did not know or care about intimately, he could not tolerate the anticipation that these underinformed citizens would condemn him to the leagues of cowards and traitors.

When the heart is squeezed, the intellect cannot always make decisions according to what O'Brien idealizes as "an act of pure reason" (*Things* 54).

Rather than make decisions inwardly—that is, trusting an internal barometer and therefore being true to ourselves—O'Brien learned that fear of public condemnation might determine what we finally do. Under the "terrible squeezing pressure" (*Things* 59) that attacks the human conscience, we can succumb to whatever society says that we must do and thus judge ourselves according to what other people say or do "as we make our choices or fail to make them" (*Things* 62). Under the "great worldwide sadness" that "came pressing down" and the "weight" that kept "pushing [him] toward the war" (*Things* 54, 59), O'Brien suffered "a moral freeze" on the Rainy River. "Canada had become a pitiful fantasy," not a solution to the pressure but a "silly and hopeless" dream of escaping his gnawing pressure:

> I couldn't decide, I couldn't act, I couldn't comport myself with even a pretense of modest human dignity. . . . Right then, with the shore so close, I understood that I would not do what I should do. I would not swim away from my hometown and my country and my life. I would not be brave. That old image of myself as a hero, as a man of conscience and courage, all that was just a threadbare pipe dream. Bobbing there on the Rainy River, looking back at the Minnesota shore, I felt a sudden swell of helplessness come over me, a drowning sensation. (*Things* 59–60)

Facing the strange and alien moment in his life when he was "ashamed of [his] conscience, ashamed to be doing the right thing" (*Things* 55), ashamed of the philosophical and political convictions that made him doubt his ability to make a moral decision ironically to fight what he believed to be an immoral war, O'Brien confesses that the boiling rivers of "hot, stupid shame" (*Things* 54) finally determined the currents of his inner struggle. National and hometown patriots would not know that they sent a "coward" to fight their war in Vietnam. "It had nothing to do with morality," good thinking, and courage, O'Brien finally writes. "I would go to the war—I would kill and maybe die—because I was embarrassed not to" (*Things* 62–63).

Although we cannot expect ideal or even rational consistency in the contemplation of courage, O'Brien learned first in the war that raged between his heart and his intellect and then in the bush of the Vietnam War "that manhood is not something to scoff at"—indeed, that "soldiering . . . is something that makes a fellow think about courage, makes a man wonder what it is and if he has it" (*If I Die* 136, 202). In the honesty of mental toughness, no man is a total hero. No man is a total coward. Working toward his own perspective on bravery, O'Brien explodes the popular cliché: "A coward dies a thousand deaths but a brave man only once." The error in this false assumption, O'Brien explains, is that no man is either "once and for always a coward" or "once and for always a hero." Operating as a foot soldier in the area of Chu Lai, including the villages of My Khe and My Lai one year after the well-known My Lai Massacre, O'Brien learned the tough reality that in the bush

> . . . men act cowardly and, at other times, act with courage, each in different measure, each with varying consistency. The men who do well on the average, perhaps with one moment of glory, those men are brave. (*If I Die* 143)

So ambiguous is the truth about courage, so intense and forgivable are the inconsistencies and contradictions of real men in crisis, a classic honor code—no matter how ideally projected, distorted, and perpetuated in gender history—deconstructs its own pressures in the hideous violence of war. In no literature about the war theater do we come to this intersection of courage more honestly than in the example of Alpha Company struggling under the fire of bullets, duty, pride, and self-preservation in *The Things They Carried*:

> For the most part they carried themselves with poise, a kind of dignity. Now and then, however, there were times of panic, when they squealed or wanted to squeal but couldn't, when they twitched and made moaning sounds and covered their heads and said Dear Jesus and flopped around on the earth and fired their weapons blindly and cringed and sobbed and begged for the noise to stop and went wild and made stupid promises to themselves and to God and to their mothers and fathers, hoping not to die. In different ways, it happened to all of them. (18–19)

Unlike the inspiring and yet coolly unrealistic cowboys, soldiers, and celebrated heroes of our childhood dreams and movies, taking fire—actually taking rounds intended to kill us, to kill the trembling flicker of perception that stands between us and dusty death—gives us vision about our vulnerability in crisis. We are never more alive, O'Brien is saying in *If I Die in a Combat Zone* and in *The Things They Carried*, than when we are almost dead. War gives us this mirror of our mortality, this truth about our humanity and courage:

> Afterward, when the firing ended, they would blink and peek up. They would touch their bodies, feeling shame, then quickly hiding it. They would force themselves to stand. As if in slow motion, frame by frame, the world would take on the old logic—absolute

silence, then the wind, then sunlight, then voices. It was the burden of being alive. Awkwardly, the men would reassemble themselves, first in private, then in groups, becoming soldiers again. They would repair the leaks in their eyes. They would check for casualties, call in dustoffs, light cigarettes, try to smile, clear their throats and spit and begin cleaning their weapons. After a time someone would shake his head and say, No lie, I almost shit my pants, and someone else would laugh, which meant it was bad, yes, but the guy had obviously not shit his pants, it wasn't that bad, and in any case nobody would ever do such a thing and then go ahead and talk about it. They would squint into the dense, oppressive sunlight. For a few moments, perhaps, they would fall silent, lighting a joint and tracking its passage from man to man, inhaling, holding in the humiliation. Scary stuff, one of them might say. But then someone else would grin or flick his eyebrows and say, Roger-dodger, almost cut me a new asshole, *almost*. (19)

Works Cited

Baker, Carlos. *Ernest Hemingway: A Life Story*. New York: Scribner's, 1969.

Brooks, Cleanth. *William Faulkner: The Yoknapatawpha County*. New Haven: Yale UP, 1963.

Hemingway, Ernest. *The Sun Also Rises*. New York: Scribner's, 1926.

O'Brien, Tim. *If I Die in a Combat Zone: Box Me up and Ship Me Home*. New York: Delta-Dell, 1989.

———. *The Things They Carried*. 1990. New York: Penguin, 1991.

Plato. "Laches." *The Collected Dialogues of Plato*. Ed. Edith Hamilton and Huntington Cairns. Bollingen Series LXXI. New York: Pantheon-Random, 1961. 123–144.

Virgil. *The Aeneid*. Trans. W. F. Jackson Knight. New York: Penguin, 1956.

CHRISTOPHER MICHAEL MCDONOUGH

"Afraid To Admit We Are Not Achilles": Facing Hector's Dilemma in Tim O'Brien's The Things They Carried

"The war, like Hector's own war, was silly and stupid."
Tim O'Brien, *If I Die in a Combat Zone*, 145

What has Troy to do with Vietnam? In recent years, the pertinence of the one Asian war to the other has been powerfully argued by numerous scholars, notably Jonathan Shay, in his seminal study, *Achilles in Vietnam: Combat Trauma and the Undoing of Character* (New York: Athenaeum, 1994), as well as by various authors responding to Shay in a special issue of *Classical Bulletin* 71.2 (1995), "Understanding Achilles." As can be seen in the titles here mentioned, the critical emphasis has generally been laid on the experience of Achilles, while little attention has focused on what James Redfield once called "the tragedy of Hector." Some discussion of the great Trojan hero might prove useful, however, especially for understanding Tim O'Brien's *The Things They Carried*, one of the finest works of American literature to emerge from the experience in Vietnam: for Hector as well as the protagonist of *The Things They Carried*, both brought to the brink by the necessity of battle, the dilemmas posed by the warrior mentality force unsettling questions about their societies and themselves.

As it was for the many young men who opposed the war in Vietnam, the debate over whether to fight or to flee had been at once a personal and political one for O'Brien. After negatively assessing the justice

From *Classical and Modern Literature* 20, no. 3 (Spring 2000): 23–32. Copyright © 1999–2000 by *Classical and Modern Literature*.

of the American involvement in Indochina, the narrator wonders whether it would be courageous or cowardly to fight for a cause he believed to be wrong. Although O'Brien elected to go to the war, the quandary remains in the foreground of his work: a central concern of *The Things They Carried*, a quasi-autobiographical work of fiction, is the shifting and indefinite line which divides bravery from cowardice (as well as honor from shame). "For the common soldier," O'Brien remarks in an oft-quoted sentence, " . . . the only certainty is overwhelming ambiguity" (88). Many literary critics have rightly characterized O'Brien's uncertainty as postmodern,[1] but in fact *The Things They Carried* deals with issues of courage as old as war itself—or at least as old as the oldest literature about war. In *If I Die in a Combat Zone*, an earlier work which anticipated many of the themes of *The Things They Carried*, O'Brien often turned to Plato for enlightenment in these matters, citing definitions of courage from both the *Laches* and the *Republic* and applying them to his own situation in Vietnam. But in *The Things They Carried*, and especially in the chapters "On the Rainy River" and "Speaking of Courage," O'Brien discusses topics which might more profitably be considered from a Homeric rather than Socratic viewpoint.

As one scholar has noted of *The Things They Carried*, "There is nothing new in what O'Brien demonstrates here about trying to tell war stories . . . and, of course, Homer's *Iliad* is the primal statement on the contradictions inherent in war."[2] Some consideration of Homer's poetry can help to sharpen analysis of combat experience as, in fact, Jonathan Shay has shown in his aforementioned study of post-traumatic stress disorder.[3] While much of *The Things They Carried* likewise deals with the subsequent effects of combat, O'Brien also assesses the soldier's frame of mind *before* going off to war: in the book's first chapter, he lists not just the assorted weapons and supplies each soldier must carry while marching, but also "the emotional baggage of men who might die" (20), thus delineating the things they carried mentally as well as physically. The contours of this state of mind are most vividly portrayed in "On the Rainy River," in which the narrator—"Tim O'Brien," a character distinct from the author—describes what he did after receiving his draft notice, in June, 1968, a few short weeks after his college graduation. At first enraged and then filled with self-pity, he spends an anxious month debating whether he should go to the war or flee his Minnesota home for Canada. One day, he snaps—a matter to be discussed more fully below—and drives north until he reaches the Rainy River; there he stops at the Tip Top Lodge, an abandoned resort on the American side of the border, run by an octogenarian named Elroy Berdahl. It is not anything which the old man says or does that is important for O'Brien during the agonizing days that follow—quite the opposite. Throughout this difficult time, the narrator is especially grateful for the "willful, almost ferocious silence" (52) Berdahl maintains, a reprieve from the pressing voices which are described at various points in the episode. Before his flight north, for instance, he had thought of what might be said by the people of his conservative hometown:

> . . . it was easy to imagine [them] sitting around a table at the old Gobbler Café on Main Street, coffee cups poised, the conversation slowly zeroing in on the young O'Brien kid, how the damned sissy had taken off for Canada. (48)

It is ultimately in these voices that O'Brien locates the source of his anxiety: in addition to a fundamental disagreement about the war in Vietnam, his dilemma is a struggle between a well-founded fear of death and a profound feeling of being ashamed. As he writes,

> Intellect had come up against emotion. My conscience told me to run, but some irrational and powerful force was resisting, like a weight pushing me toward the war. What it came down to, stupidly, was a sense of shame. Hot, stupid shame. I did not want people to think badly of me. Not my parents, not my brother and sister, not even the folks down at the Gobbler Café. (54)

To be at odds with public opinion was not an unusual position in 1968, to be sure. But while it would be wrong to reduce O'Brien's objections to the war to the mere desire to save his own skin, his remarks nonetheless take on meaningful perspective when compared with several episodes in the *Iliad* centering on the intertwined notions of glory and shame.

In his ground-breaking study, *The Greeks and the Irrational*, E. R. Dodds has noted, "Homeric man's highest good is not the enjoyment of a quiet con-science, but the enjoyment of time, public esteem."[4] This is not to say that the warriors at Troy are mindless automata surrendering all individuality to the whims of the crowd: in fact, they are acutely aware that the needs of the self and the demands of society may well be in conflict. James Redfield aptly puts it, "All men are born to die, but the warrior alone must confront this fact in his social life . . . The greatness of Homer's heroes is a greatness not of act but of consciousness."[5] There is a direct relationship in Homer's world between the risks one is willing to run and the respect society will confer; for this reason, the battlefield, where the threat to life is greatest, is the hero's proving ground. It is important to realize that the hero's status depends upon (and, in fact, cannot exist without) the tension between personal and public impulses: this tension is at the center of the epic. "The wrath of Achilles"—the words with which the *Iliad* famously opens—is directed not at the Trojans but at Agamemnon, the commander who has arbitrarily stripped him of his war-bride, Briseis. As a woman, Briseis means little to the hero, but as a prize he has legitimately earned for valor in battle, her significance is immense. In this foolish exercise of power, Agamemnon unintentionally sets into motion a crisis about the nature of heroism which brings Achilles face-to-face with the hollowness of his shame culture: why should there be any personal risk, if there is to be no public recognition?[6]

In addition to the possibility of winning glory, the Homeric hero is motivated also by *aidos,* "shame." By and large, this aspect of the ancient mentality is typified in the person of Hector, Achilles' great Trojan opponent.[7] More than any other combatant at Troy, Hector is aware of his special status as a warrior: as the greatest hero on the Trojan side, he carries the greatest burden in its defense and has the greatest reputation to lose in any defeat. Nonetheless, Hector is only mortal and cannot overcome Achilles, the son of a goddess; Achilles' withdrawal, however, allows Hector to score enormous victories over the Greeks, culminating in the slaying of Patroclus. When Achilles subsequently rejoins the battle, Hector has grown proud in his achievements and so ignores the advice of his brother Polydamas that he remove the troops from the field. What follows is a complete disaster for the Trojans: those who escape slaughter run headlong back to Troy, leaving Hector alone in Book Twenty-two to face the all-but-invincible Achilles. There, before the gates of Troy as the whole city watches from the walls, harsh reality begins to set in on Hector, who says to himself (22.99–110),

> Ah me, if I go now inside the gates and wall, Polydamas will be
> the first to reproach me, since he tried to convince me to lead the
> Trojans back to the city on that fateful night when godlike Achilles
> rose up. But I would not listen, though it would have been far better
> had I. Now since I have by my own stupidity destroyed my people,
> I am ashamed before the Trojans and the Trojan women in their
> trailing robes, that some lesser man than I will say of me, *Hector*
> *put his faith in his own strength, and destroyed his people.* That is what
> they will say. But for me, it would be much better then to confront
> Achilles, strike him down, and return, or else to be killed by him in
> glory before the city.

Generations of readers have rightly admired the determination of Hector to see this heroic challenge through to its fatal end; O'Brien himself writes in *If I Die in a Combat Zone* how hard it is to picture oneself "as the eternal Hector, dying gallantly" (146). Hector's refusal to retreat, however, must not be judged according to a reductive concept of bravery, but rather in terms of competing disincentives, as identified succinctly by Redfield: "Hector's fear of death is overcome by his greater fear of disgrace."[8]

Although a very different set of political circumstances stands in the background, a similar fear of disgrace overtakes O'Brien as he agonizes on the Rainy River. Like Hector who envisions the ridicule of the Trojans, he imagines his entire community watching and yelling at him, an overwhelming sensation he cannot endure. "I would go to the war," he writes, "—I would kill and maybe die—because I was embarrassed not to" (62). Perhaps somewhat harshly, O'Brien calls himself a coward for giving in to these voices; he knows, though, that he has only chosen the lesser of his fears, stating earlier in the book of soldiers in general, "It was not courage, exactly; the object was not valor. Rather, they were too frightened to be cowards" (21). These thoughts are handled more fully in "Under the Mountain," a chapter from *If I Die in a Combat Zone*, in which the narrator's friend Erik discusses Ezra Pound's "Hugh Selwyn Mauberley" while the pair are still in boot camp at Fort Lewis, Washington. "All this not because of conviction, not for ideology," Erik says,

> rather it's from fear of society's censure, just as Pound claims. Fear of weakness. Fear that to avoid war is to avoid manhood. We come to Fort Lewis afraid to admit we are not Achilles, that we are not brave, not heroes. (45)

As a consideration of the theoretical roots of heroism shows, the warrior's status is etched round by fears: it is only a matter of which one to give in to, or *not* to give in to, as the case may be. In Book Twenty-two, Hector is quite literally backed up against a wall. Before him lies Achilles and certain doom, behind him the Trojans and intolerable derision. Although he toys temporarily with the fantasy of a settlement, between these options there really is no other—he can be either a dead hero or a live coward. But at the crucial moment, as Achilles bears down, Hector runs. It would be a misinterpretation to see this as the cowardly choice, for it is neither cowardly nor a choice: we must note that, caught between difficult options, Hector does not run back *inside* the walls of Troy but instead *around* them, in this way straddling the line between death and dishonor. Eventually, the goddess Athena fools him into thinking his brother has joined him for the fight; he stops, realizes the trick, and is killed. Nonetheless, Homer's portrait of Hector powerfully captures the unyielding nature of the heroic paradox: the poet renders the warrior's inability to decide in terms of a mad dash around a wall.

Something like this Homeric trope of indecision—Hector's going around in circles—is to be found in O'Brien's work, where it symbolizes much the same thing. In *If I Die in a Combat Zone*, for instance, he writes that, after getting his draft notice in 1968, "Late at night, the town deserted, two or three of us would drive a car around and around the town's lake, talking about the war . . ." (25). O'Brien has employed this image several times in his work, most notably in "Speaking of Courage" from *The Things They Carried*. In this vignette, the narrator's friend, Norman Bowker, having returned home from the war, spends the Fourth of July driving his father's car around a lake eleven times pondering an important failure of nerve he had experienced in Vietnam. In both places, O'Brien patterns the decision between cowardice or courage in terms much like Hector's run, as a repeated circular motion.[9]

Closer still in spirit to Hector's dilemma is O'Brien's own flight to the Canadian border in "On the Rainy River." Throughout the difficult time after getting his draft notice, the narrator feels in himself "a moral split," an overwhelming sensation which, though eventually growing to encompass the world around him, originates in a simple dichotomy: "Run, I'd think. Then I'd think, Impossible. Then a second later I'd think, *Run*." As he continues, "I feared the war, yes, but I also feared exile" (48).[10] Later in the summer, this sense of internal division manifests itself externally, when one day, as he remarks, "I felt something break open in my chest. . . . a physical rupture—a cracking-leaking-popping feeling" (49). As a result of this crisis—quite literally a breaking point—O'Brien suddenly takes off, driving north until he reaches Elroy Berdahl's Tip Top Lodge. When O'Brien first sees the old man, his sense of self-division is all the more reinforced, since Berdahl carries a small paring knife, and furthermore, as he notes,

> His eyes had the bluish gray color of a razor blade, the same polished shine, and as he peered up at me I felt a strange sharpness, almost painful, a cutting sensation, as if his gaze were somehow slicing me open. (51)

While the narrator acknowledges that this sensation is a result in part of guilt, we might also see his description of Berdahl's gaze as the widening of his problem from the personal to the cosmic. So great is the crisis which O'Brien feels—so strong is his sense of the dilemma facing him—that he feels it is visible to the people he meets. Indeed, this "moral split" which has already affected his body he now even senses in the landscape, as he waits for resolution by "the Rainy River, which separates Minnesota from Canada, and which for me separated one life from another" (50).

It is in this ambivalent region, poised between conflicting visions of his future—balanced precariously at the Tip Top, as it were—that O'Brien wrestles with his conscience. Here, where he describes himself as "half awake, half dreaming," his riven mental state is figured strongly by his liminal status: we might recognize that the dilemma which Hector in the *Iliad* faced (and never resolved for himself) was rendered in topographical terms, as it is here by O'Brien, who envisions himself "on the margins of exile," and "[g]etting chased by the Border Patrol" (53).[11] At this excruciating point in the narrative, Elroy Berdahl takes O'Brien out for a fishing trip on the highly symbolic Rainy River. As the small motorboat makes its way upstream, O'Brien realizes "that at some point we must've passed into Canadian waters, across that dotted line between two different worlds" (58). The narrator surmises that, in bringing the situation to this point, Berdahl had taken him "to the edge" and would watch "as I chose a life for myself" (58). He chooses Vietnam rather than Canada—that is, fight rather than flight—making the same decision Hector did, though by surviving, he avoids Hector's fate. In forcing O'Brien's decision between the difficult options before him, Berdahl reenacts the role which Athena had played in Hector's final moments, though the old man with the sharp gray eyes is more benevolent to his charge than the gray-eyed goddess had been. "He was a witness, like God, or like the gods," writes O'Brien, "who look on in absolute silence as we live our lives, as we make our choices or fail to make them" (62).

Though these gods seem more Lucretian than Homeric, perhaps the author has consciously drawn on the *Iliad* for these remarks. In this context, it is worth noting Homer's description of the divine audience watching Hector's final moments (22.158–166):

> It was a great man who fled, but far better he who pursued him rapidly, since here was no festal beast, no ox-hide they strove for, which are the prizes that are given men for racing. No, they are running for the life of Hector, breaker of horses. As when about the turnposts racehorses with uncloven hooves run at full speed, since a great prize is laid up for their winning, a tripod or a woman, in games for a man's funeral, so these two swept whirling about the city of Priam in the speed of their feet, while all the gods were looking upon them.

As his moment of crisis, O'Brien feels that he too is surrounded by a roaring stadium crowd "[l]ike some weird sporting event" (60), and that the gaze of a civic pantheon which includes Abraham Lincoln, Saint George, the U.S. Senate, and LBJ, falls upon him. Numbered among these cultural luminaries is "a blind poet scribbling notes" (60). Very likely this description refers to Robert Frost's famous reading at the inauguration of President Kennedy, but does not the epithet "blind" also bring to mind the blind poet of Chios, Homer himself?

As an issue of interpretation, however, it can hardly matter whether or not O'Brien alludes deliberately to Homer. Because all wars result in widespread destruction and death, survivors "shape their own discoveries of war into patterns first to be found in Homer," as classicist James Tatum once noted in *The Yale Review*.[12] Both Homer and O'Brien portray the experience of those who must come to grips with the dilemma courage imposes: on the one hand is the loss of face, on the other, the loss of life. For Homer, the debate which rages within Hector's heart about these difficulties is dramatized as a race around the walls of a city which his hero cannot honorably enter. This same debate is felt inside Tim O'Brien's heart as well and manifests itself bodily, growing so large at last that it requires the natural and political boundary dividing a continent to describe it. In each work, the authors imagine such divisions of self in broadly geographical terms, as their protagonists negotiate the no-man's land between the antitheses described by O'Brien so well: "War makes you a man; war makes you dead" (*The Things They Carried*, 87).

Notes

* Works of Tim O'Brien which will be referred to infra are: *The Things They Carried: A Work of Fiction* (Boston: Houghton Mifflin, 1990) and *If I Die in a Combat Zone, Box Me Up and Ship Me Home* (New York: Dell Pub. Co., 1973). Translations from Greek are the author's own. For their help with this piece, the author would like to thank Kelly Malone, David Gill, S.J., and *CML*'s editor and anonymous referee.

1. See Steven Kaplan, *Understanding Tim O'Brien* (Columbia: U of South Carolina Pr, 1995), 169–192; Don Ringnalda, *Fighting and Writing the Vietnam War* (Jackson: University Pr of Mississippi, 1994), 90–114; and Catherine Calloway, "'How to Tell a True War Story': Metafiction in *The Things They Carried*," *Critique* 36 (1995): 249–257. For a recent Marxist critique of this postmodern position, see Jim Neilson, *Warring Fictions: American Literary Culture and the Vietnam War Narrative* (Jackson: University Pr of Mississippi, 1998), 191–209.

2. Kaplan (above, note 1) 185.

3. O'Brien has called Shay's book "one of the most original and most important scholarly works to have emerged from the Vietnam war," although he does not consider his own work to be therapeutic (1990: 179).

4. E. R. Dodds, *The Greeks and the Irrational* (Berkeley: U of California Pr, 1951), 17.

5. James M. Redfield, *Nature and Culture in the* Iliad: *The Tragedy of Hector*, enlarged edition (Durham: Duke U Pr, 1994), 101.

6. See Achilles' famous response to Odysseus, *Iliad* 9.307–429, especially 318–322.

7. See Redfield (above, note 5) 119, who notes, "Hector is a warrior not because he loves war but because he is before all else a hero of *aidos*."

8. Redfield (above, note 5) 115.

9. The various revisions of "Speaking of Courage" have been expertly charted by Mark Taylor, "Tim O'Brien's War," *The Centennial Review* 39 (Summer 1995): 213–230, who notes that the

circles around the lake suggest the endlessness and purposelessness of the Vietnam War to those who fought it . . . and the undifferentiated moments of life afterwards for many veterans. These circles also suggest O'Brien's going round and round the central events of his own wartime experience, and of his imagination, working tirelessly to get it right, to find the truth, to display the meaning he wishes to display. (218)

10. On exile in O'Brien's work, see especially Tina Chen, "'Unraveling the Deeper Meaning': Exile and the Embodied Poetics of Displacement in Tim O'Brien's *The Things They Carried*," *Contemporary Literature* 39 (1998): 77–98.

11. Ringnalda (above, note 1) 101–102 has explicated "On the Rainy River" as a description of "liminal uncertainty" conveying the ambiguity between genres of truth and fiction. Typically, Ringnalda overstates his case: "O'Brien knows that reality is accessible *only* through mediation. That being the case, he spurns the Western paradigm of Manichaean dualism, which convinces most of the people most of the time that they can tell the difference between reality and fiction" (104). Is Manichaean dualism really "Western"? See the penetrating critique of Neilson (above, note 1) 200–203 on this point.

12. James Tatum, "The *Iliad* and Memories of War," *The Yale Review* 76 (1986): 16.

PAMELA SMILEY

The Role of the Ideal (Female) Reader in Tim O'Brien's The Things They Carried: Why Should Real Women Play?

Tim O'Brien (narrator) visits Jimmy Cross (character) years after both have returned from Vietnam. They drink gin, swap memories and look at snapshots of that time when they were both "incredibly soft and young" (29). One photo is the volleyball shot of gray-eyed Martha whom Jimmy Cross loves, but who responded to his expressed intention to carry her upstairs and tie her to his bed (where he'd spend the night touching her knee) by crossing her arms protectively across her chest and saying she didn't "understand how men could do those things . . . the things men do" (31).

As O'Brien leaves, Jimmy Cross gives him permission to tell his stories only if they make Cross such a hero that Martha will "read [them] and come begging."

> "Make me out to be a good guy, huh? Brave and handsome, all that stuff. Best platoon leader ever." He hesitated for a second. "And do me a favor. Don't mention anything about ____."
> "No," I said. "I won't." (31)

Herein lies the central project of O'Brien's *The Things They Carried*: to make the Marthas who stayed home during the sixties and seventies playing volleyball, going to college, reading Virginia Woolf, to make such women

From *The Massachusetts Review* 43, no. 4 (Winter 2002–2003): 602–13. Copyright © 2003 by *The Massachusetts Review*.

understand their brothers, friends and lovers who went to Vietnam. This O'Brien (the author) accomplishes through a series of female characters—Martha, Mary Ann, Lemon's sister, the woman at the reading, and Linda—through whom he de-genders war, constructs an ideal (female) reader, and re-defines American masculinity.

War fiction is usually less concerned with women than with rituals and tests that "make you a man" (87). The plotting of these—in novels, film, and popular culture—follows genre conventions. First is the separation from women and their "civilizing" influence. Second is the performance of masculinity according to traditional standards involving bravery, physical prowess, and virility. And third is the company of men, particularly the wizened sergeant (or some other father figure) who pronounces the young soldier "a man."

For example, Nick Adams from *In Our Time* (one of the Oedipal works against which *The Things They Carried* plays out its Bloomsian anxiety of influence) wants to silence women having babies, be free of the responsibilities Marjorie brings with her, and be left alone to perform stoically in Seney's burned wasteland. Once separated from women, figures like Rambo (another example) can be pulled from the primordial slime ("look at those pecs! How could that be anything BUT a real man?") to reassure moviegoers that despite the moral swamp of Vietnam and its consequent feminization of America, figures of uncompromised masculinity still exist. (See Jeffords' "Masculinity as Excess" for an analysis of this dynamic in Vietnam War films.)

Interestingly, *The Things They Carried* departs radically from these conventions. Mary Ann, in Vietnam, not only fails to "civilize," but is herself seduced by the war. It is not to a company of men that O'Brien's characters perform, but rather to ideal readers in the form of Lemon's sister and the woman at the reading. And instead of an act of uncompromised masculinity signaling the boy is now a man, O'Brien's character appropriates the feminine, becoming an androgynous fusion of preadolescent Timmy and Linda.

Mary Ann

Against the figure of Martha who crosses her arms against understanding "the things men do," stands Mary Ann, "the sweetheart of Song Tra Bong." Are women less warlike than men because they have breasts and give birth? Mary Ann is O'Brien's argument that the kinder, gentler world of the feminine is nothing but an illusion. As Rat Kiley puts it:

> You got these blinders on about women. How gentle and peaceful they are. All that crap about how if we had a pussy for president

there would be no more war. Pure garbage. You got to get rid of that sexist attitude. (117)

Women who never go to war are not innocent so much as they are ignorant of their own capacity for violence. Mary Ann is a test case. She comes to Vietnam right out of high school in "white culottes and this sexy pink sweater": a cliché of the American girl and the female equivalent of Jimmy Cross, Curt Lemon, Kiowa, and the narrator. By the time Mary Ann disappears in the shadows of the jungle, her face is "smooth and vacant" and she wears a "necklace of human tongues" (125).

Mary Ann explains her own awakening in terms of appetite and carnal excitement, of being absolutely in the body.

> Sometimes I want to eat this place. Vietnam. I want to swallow the whole country—the dirt, death—I just want to eat it and have it there inside me . . . When I'm out there at night, I feel close to my own body. I can feel my blood moving, my skin and my fingernails, everything. It's like I'm full of electricity and I'm glowing in the dark—I'm on fire almost—I'm burning away into nothing—but it doesn't matter because I know exactly who I am. You can't feel like that anywhere else. (121)

Notice, in contrast, how the (male?) narrator of "How to Tell a True War Story" describes his reaction to war. He does not appetitively ingest the world, does not lose his sense of himself as subject, and instead of a heightened sense of embodiment, feels "out-of-his-skin."

> After a firefight, there is always an immense pleasure of aliveness. The trees are alive. The grass, the soil—everything. All around you things are purely living, and you among them. And the aliveness makes you tremble. You feel an intense, out-of-the-skin awareness of your living self—your truest self, the human being you want to be and then become by force of wanting it. (87)

While it is interesting that O'Brien has his female character taking the world inside her and his male character expanding out to become the world, his point seems to be less the gender stereotypes than the (non-gendered) Dionysian energy common to both descriptions. War destroys order, subverts higher processes such as reason and compassion, and returns us to instinct and our bodies. Such an explosive release allows men and women to be what they might have been without cultural restraints. This O'Brien notes:

A true war story is never moral. It does not instruct nor encourage
virtue, nor suggest models of proper human behavior, nor restrain
men from doing things men have always done. (76)

Mary Ann illustrates not just the release war brings, but also how women
(and this is gender-specific) are "freed" when they travel outside of their culture and its definitions of what it means to be a woman. Think of Isak Dine-
sen and Beryl Markham and Alexandra David-Neel. This is true especially
in Asia, where Western women are accorded the status of honorary men. For
Mary Ann such freedom allows her to explore appetite and power—a matrix
that has proved a rich vein for feminist exploration. (See, for example, Susan
Bordo's *Unbearable Weight*.)

Mary Ann confesses to an appetite so large she could "swallow the
whole country." Uncontained woman's appetite=chaos: O'Brien defuses such
an equation by couching Mary Ann's appetite in terms of heterosexual sex
and pregnancy. Even her necklace of human tongues doesn't carry the horror
it could; rather, as is consistent with the rest of *The Things They Carried*, its
violence is seen at a slant. Azar straps a grenade to a puppy. Rat shoots a baby
water buffalo. Lemon steals nightgowns from Mama-sans. The only contact
with the enemy ends in "the man I killed," a source of grief for the narrator,
not a passage into manhood.

Underlying each of the acts listed above, however, is a more serious violence, the unspeakable "_____" Jimmy Cross makes the narrator promise not to
include. Killing, destruction, rape: the very stuff of the war genre is missing in
O'Brien. Mary Ann demonstrates that woman, by virtue of her female body,
is not immune to "that mix of unnamed terror and unnamed pleasure that
comes as the needle slips in and you know you're risking something" (125), a
demonstration that might collapse should Jimmy Cross' "_____" be too explicitly filled. In fact, Mary Ann is less persuasive as an argument that "women
do these things, too" than she is as an example of "those of us who have done
these things are still human; given the situation you'd have done the same."
This argument "human, just like you" shifts the normative masculine away
from a lethal Dionysian erotic energy to the benign wantonness Azar claims
in self-defense: "Christ, I'm just a boy" (40). In post-Vietnam America, masculinity released from the constraints of feminine civilization moves not to
Rambo or John Wayne but to Mary Ann and Timmy.

Lemon's Sister and the Older Woman at the Reading
One such "_____" O'Brien elides to avoid the usual stuff of war is Curt
Lemon's trick-or-treating. The several tellings of the story and the reaction
of Lemon's sister to one version allow O'Brien to construct his ideal reader (a

female) through the negative example of the "dumb cooze who never writes back" (76).

Rat Kiley writes a letter to Curt Lemon's sister to tell her "what a great brother she had, how together the guy was, a number one pal and comrade. A real soldier's soldier" (75). Kiley's impulse is the same as Jimmy Cross' "read them and come begging": to use storytelling to win a female reader.

Except that Kiley has not learned the value of "____." He tells this version of Lemon's trick-or-treating in a letter to the dead man's sister:

> On Halloween, this really hot spooky night, the dude paints his body all different colors and puts on this weird mask and hikes over to the ville and goes trick or treating almost stark naked, just boots and balls and an M-16. (76)

A man lurking in the shadows, the conflation of sexuality and violence ("balls and an M-16"), nakedness: these are the details of a rape. Susan Griffin (for one) argues that the real difference between men and women's embodiment is women's constant vigilance against rape, a condition to which Kiley's details betray no sensitivity.

O'Brien, the narrator who is "too smart, too compassionate, too every-thing . . . A liberal, for Christ's sake" (45) intervenes and explains Kiley:

> He is nineteen years old and it is too much for him—so he looks at you with those big sad gentle killer eyes and says cooze because his friend is dead, and because it's so incredibly sad and true: she never wrote back. (76–7)

Kiley is the victim: victim of his youth, the press of history, his killer eyes, and of the woman who never wrote back.

Fictionalized acts of reading often signal what an author requires of his/her ideal reader. Here, the "dumb cooze" is a negative example: the ideal woman reader will not be squeamish about sexual violence and will remain open to con-fessional male voices, particularly those with "sad gentle killer eyes." To judge Lemon is to take Martha's position: crossed arms, refusing to "understand . . . the things men do." To not judge is to be open, like Mary Ann.

O'Brien does not deny the subtext of sexual violence. In a later re-telling of the trick-or-treat story Kiley makes explicit the previously implicit female victim.

> See what happens is, it's like four in the morning and Lemon sneaks into a hootch with the weird ghost mask on. Everyone's

asleep, right? So he wakes up this cute little Mama-san. Tickles her foot. "Hey Mama-san," he goes, real soft-like. "Hey Mama-san, trick-or-treat!" Should've seen her face. About freaks. I mean there's this buck naked ghost standing there and he's got this M-16 against her ear and he whispers "Hey Mama-san, trick-or-fucking-treat!" Then he takes off her p.j.s. Strips her right down. Sticks the pajamas in his sack and tucks her into bed and heads for the next hootch. (286)

Rather than deny the violence of Jimmy Cross' "____," O'Brien mitigates it by including other—equally masculine, but often overlooked—"things men do." Jimmy Cross holding a pebble under his tongue. The sunlight lifting Lemon into the canopy of trees. The buzz of the mountains coining alive at sunset. These are the details of a seduction. The seduction of the female reader who must be aware of, at the same time she suspends judgment on, the "____."

"Don't ever mention _____:"
"No" I said. "I won't." (31)

"How to Tell a True War Story" has another female character, "always a woman. Usually it's an older woman of kindly temperament and humane politics" (90). This character, too, is caught by a story, O'Brien's reading of Rat Kiley's killing of the baby water buffalo.

[Rat Kiley] stepped back and shot it through the front knee. The animal did not make a sound. It went down hard, then got up again, and Rat took careful aim and shot off an ear. He shot it twice in the hindquarters and in the little hump at its back . . . It wasn't to kill; it was to hurt . . . Curt Lemon was dead. Rat Kiley had lost his best friend in the world . . . But for now it was a question of pain. (65)

Fury and the blind impulse to cause pain are part of the experience of war. For O'Brien to not include them would strain credibility, but it is his method of detailing these things that distinguishes him. The baby buffalo moment is similar to one of the most disturbing scenes in the movie *Platoon*, in which American soldiers destroy a Vietnamese village after finding their friend crucified on the trail. In O'Brien, the fury is directed at the baby buffalo rather than a village of people, displacing some of the horror while not denying it. And yet the narrator is still acutely sensitive to the reader holding herself apart and judging. The older woman who hears the story explains

> That as a rule she hates war stories; cannot understand why people want to wallow in all the blood and gore. But this one she liked. The poor baby water buffalo, it made her sad. (90)

And the narrator counters that she has not listened. Her sensibility is misplaced. She doesn't get it because the story is "about sunlight . . . It's about love and memory" (91).

She has reduced this complex paradox to a cliché of pop self-help psychology. He must, she advises, simply leave it behind and get on with life.

The older woman, like the dumb cooze, is a fictionalized act of reading whereby O'Brien fashions his ideal reader. Jimmy Cross wants Martha to hear his stories and accept them. Rat Kiley wants Lemon's sister to read and understand. O'Brien wants the older woman to hear his love story. Mitchell Sanders generalizes beyond the female reader, but even he eventually circles back and identifies her as his central audience. She is the one who counts.

> Nobody listens. Nobody hears nothin'. Like that fatass colonel. The politicians, all the civilian types. Your girlfriend. My girlfriend. Everybody's sweet little virgin girlfriend. (83)

When a woman listens and understands, something shifts. As a result, the man's experience has—what is it? Reality? Validity? Redemption? Instead of the sergeant who proclaims the soldier a man, it is the ideal female reader for whom O'Brien's characters perform their masculinity.

Linda

Zen-like paradoxes shape this work. "War stories are love stories." "Truth is a lie." A woman is a "virgin and not a virgin." It is no surprise then that O'Brien resolves the collection's project—making the Marthas of the world understand; constructing the ideal female reader; giving the male protagonist's experience validity, reality and redemption—through paradox as well. In the final story, "Lives of the Dead" (the title itself a paradox), the narrator pushes each of his previous points to that space outside of the logic we collectively hold to be true. Not only are women (Mary Ann) capable of doing what men do, but also despite men doing the things they do, they remain innocents. Not only does O'Brien construct an ideal female reader, he becomes her in Linda. And redemption lies not in the sergeant's or reader's or lover's witness, but in the very act of creation, the "loops and spins and . . . high leaps" of storytelling (273).

O'Brien's narrative success at repressing the usual elements of war—killing, rape, destruction—prepares the way for him to claim that despite the fact that he has killed a man and lived through Vietnam's "Garden of Evil. Over here, man, every sin's real fresh and original" (86), he remains Timmy, his innocent childhood self. The man finds himself in the boy he was, and that self hasn't "changed at all. I was Timmy then; now I'm Tim" (265).

At the end of the twentieth century, the meaning of manhood in America is anything but straightforward. Susan Faludi's *Stiffed* is only the most recent in an ongoing conversation that includes *Harper's* cover article, "Are Men Necessary?", the Promise Keepers, Robert Bly, and the Million Man March. This crisis began, some claim, with the Vietnam War generation. Traditional rituals of passage possible for soldiers in World Wars I and II were no longer available to their sons and grandsons. The average age of the "boys" in Vietnam was eighteen.

Manhood, for O'Brien's narrator, is a return to the boy he was. And that boy contains Linda, the girl he loved when he was nine. Now, at forty-three, he speaks to her in dreams, tells her story, imagines her alive.

> And then it becomes 1990. I'm forty-three years old, and a writer now, still dreaming Linda alive in exactly the same way. She's not embodied Linda; she's mostly made up, with a new identity and a new name, like the man who never was . . . [I]n the spell of memory and imagination, I can still see her as if through ice, as if I'm gazing into some other world, a place where there are no bodies at all. I can see Kiowa, too, and Ted Lavender and Curt Lemon and sometimes I can even see Timmy skating with Linda under the yellow floodlights. (273)

Unlike Martha who crosses her arms or the dumb cooze who never wrote back, Linda cannot hold herself apart because she is frozen, static, she is Timmy. Her allure is her link to all that is best in Tim. Her threat is the stink of death she carries, the inevitable end of every body. It is usually, Julia Kristeva's "Stabat Mater" argues, women's position to stand between man and death. While this role has a place in *The Things They Carried* (Dobbins with his girlfriend's pantyhose around his neck even after the woman drops him: "no sweat . . . The magic doesn't go away" [130]), it is not where O'Brien ends up.

The skating rink's invitation to self-knowledge gestures toward Walden Pond, the tarn near the House of Usher, Ahab's ocean, and the swamp of the Big Two-hearted River. But it's frozen water: a mirror as well as a transparent barrier that both links and separates O'Brien from the dead on whose lives he writes in order to protect Timmy.

> I'm young and I'll never die. I'm skimming across the surface of my own history, moving fast, riding the melt beneath the blades, doing loops and spins, and when I take high leaps into the dark and come down thirty years later, I realize it's Tim trying to save Timmy's life with a story. (273)

"I'll never die." These are the very words the young boy in Hemingway's "Indian Camp" believes when he returns with his father (a doctor) from a particularly difficult birthing.

> They were seated in the boat, Nick in the stern, his father rowing. The sun was coming over the hills. A bass jumped, making a circle in the water. Nick trailed his hand in the water. It felt warm in the sharp chill of the morning. In the early morning on the lake sitting in the stern of the boat with his father rowing, he felt quite sure that he would never die. ("Indian Camp" 19)

Both Hemingway and O'Brien evoke the moment at which the boy enters the secret circle of manhood. The difference is that Hemingway's character leaves the woman behind in the Indian camp, O'Brien's freezes her and makes the ice the surface on which the protective circle of manhood is composed.

In the final paragraph of O'Brien's collection, Linda lies frozen beneath the ice on which O'Brien "loops and spins" his stories. "Not dead," Linda explains in a dream. "But when I am, it's like ... I don't know, I guess it's like being inside a book nobody's reading" (273). Linda's death, O'Brien's absorption of and recreation of her, the self-protective distance denied the "dumb cooze": these "____" aren't a whole lot different from woman as blank sheet, nature fashioned into culture, the raw stuff of men's art—all those boringly familiar and too predictable functions of women's place in men's art. Too obvious to even deserve comment.

More interesting is the question, why do women readers play? Why would any woman reader want to become O'Brien's ideal, given the conditions he sets? The answer, I believe, lies not so much in the genre of war literature as it does in the gothic.

At the climax of the gothic, the hero (heretofore a public figure of great power who has amused himself by torturing and toying with a female innocent, the protagonist) realizes the woman he has been victimizing is not peripheral to his life, but its very center. She is his soul. His meaning. And he surrenders to her. A Heathcliffian love.

As in all effective gothics, the love in *The Things They Carried* is at once both hotly sexual and intensely spiritual. Jimmy Cross wants to

Sleep inside [Martha's] lungs and breathe her blood. Be smothered. He wanted her to be a virgin and not a virgin all at once. He wanted to know her intimate secrets . . . (12)

And nine-year-old Timmy "wanted to live inside [Linda's] body. I wanted to melt into her bones—that kind of love" (258).

This fusion of woman and man is not the stuff of Woodstock and the casual sex of the Pill. This is not daily shopping lists and three o'clock feedings and the toilet seat (up? down?). This is a love of epic proportions in which soul mates merge and their union contains everything. In an age that takes sex and love so lightly, this is an exceptional claim to make for the love of a woman. That she is the means of spiritual redemption. That only through her can life become whole. No wonder O'Brien writes, "It wasn't a war story. It was a love story" (90). No wonder women read him. Where else in post-Vietnam American culture is a woman's love worth so much?

WORKS CITED

Susan Griffin, "Rape and the Power of Consciousness" in *Issues in Feminism*. Ed. Sheila Ruth. London: Mayfield Publishers 1995, 285–295.

Ernest Hemingway, "Indian Camp" from *In Our Time*. New York: Collier Books, 1925.

Susan Jeffords, "Masculinity as Excess in Vietnam Films: The Father–Son Dynamic of American Culture" in *Feminisms: An Anthology of Literary Theory and Criticism*. Ed. Robyn R. Warhol and Diane Price Herndl. New Brunswick, New Jersey: Rutgers UP, 1991.

Julia Kristeva, "Stabat Mater," in *Tales of Love*. Trans. Leon S. Roudiez. New York: Columbia University Press, 1987.

Tim O'Brien, *The Things They Carried: A Work of Fiction*. Boston: Houghton Mifflin, 1990.

SUSAN FARRELL

Tim O'Brien and Gender:
A Defense of The Things They Carried

Alongside the popularity and critical acclaim awarded the outpouring of recent U.S. accounts of the Vietnam War sit some more quietly voiced criticisms of this body of literature. Perhaps the most compelling of these critiques has emerged from recent feminist scholars who argue that much Vietnam War literature replicates traditional Western notions of gender and thus reinforces patriarchal institutions and beliefs. Two key works published in 1989 set the stage for much of the feminist criticism of Vietnam War literature that was to follow. Susan Jeffords' *The Remasculinization of America: Gender and the Vietnam War* (1989) explores popular film and narrative representations of the war. Jeffords argues for reading the war as a "construction of gendered interests," despite the fact that war might initially seem to be the domain of men and not relevant to gender analysis (81). A special issue of the journal *Vietnam Generation* devoted to the topic of gender and the war also appeared in 1989. In her introduction to this special issue, editor Jacqueline Lawson responds to a much-read *Esquire* article by ex-Marine William Broyles, Jr., "Why Men Love War." While Broyles claims that "war is the enduring condition of man, period," Lawson writes that she hopes this issue of the journal will dispel such a "canard—that war is the exclusive province of men, a closed and gendered activity inscribed by myth, informed by ritual, and enacted solely through the power relations of patriarchy" (6).

From *The CEA Critic* 66, no. 1 (Fall 2003): 1–21. Copyright © 2003 by the College English Association.

To this end, she has explored some of the brutal rape and torture scenes of Vietnamese women that occur regularly in the literature.

Similarly, critic Maria Bonn has argued convincingly that Michael Herr's critically acclaimed account of the war, *Dispatches*, "confirms war as a masculine experience" by using a language which conflates military and sexual conquest (37). Critic Lorrie Smith has added to the debate, pointing out that "most popular treatments of the war—for all their claims to 'tell it like it was'—reveal more about the cultural and political climate of the 1980s than about the war itself" ("Back" 115). Smith connects a 1980s backlash against the feminist movement to the misogyny she reads in Vietnam War literature, a misogyny which she describes as "very visible," as seemingly "natural and expected." In popular representations, Smith argues, the "Vietnam War is being reconstructed as a site where white American manhood—figuratively as well as literally wounded during the war and assaulted by the women's movement for twenty years—can reassert its dominance in the social hierarchy" ("Back" 115).

The work of Tim O'Brien, while highly praised, has not been exempt from the criticism of feminist scholars. Lorrie Smith argues that the short fiction that eventually came together to make up *The Things They Carried* silences women and re-enforces traditional masculine views of war and gender. Smith writes that O'Brien's "text offers no challenge to a discourse of war in which apparently innocent American men are tragically wounded and women are objectified, excluded, and silenced" ("Things" 17). While Smith points out that her intent "is not to devalue O'Brien's technical skill or emotional depth," she does want to "account for [her] own discomfort as a female reader and to position *The Things They Carried* within a larger cultural project to rewrite the Vietnam War from a masculinist and strictly American perspective" (17). She argues that, even though O'Brien's narrator says that only those who were there can fully understand the events which occurred, he still permits a bond to form between male readers and the characters on the basis that women are completely unable to understand "the things men do." Male readers become less marked as outsiders than women as the stories progress since "the shared language of patriarchy" eases the general incommunicability of the war trauma for men (19).

Smith supports her argument with a close reading of both the longer stories that first appeared in *Esquire* magazine and the shorter vignettes that O'Brien added when he collected the material as a book. She argues that the opening, title story of the collection "establishes a pattern . . . for the rest of the book" in that it teaches readers that survival in war depends on "suppressing femininity" (24). Readers learn, as does Lieutenant Jimmy Cross, that the renunciation of the feminine, is "a sad but necessary cost of war" (24). Martha in the opening story, along with women like Sally Gustafson, Curt Lemon's sister, the well-intentioned older woman who cries for the baby water buffalo in "How to Tell a True War Story," and the narrator's daughter Kathleen all represent another world: those back home who will never understand the war. Even more, this inability to understand is at least partly willful: they do not understand because they do not listen. According to Smith, O'Brien's particular emphasis on women not listening "preserve[s] the absolute dichotomy of masculinity and femininity and perpetuate[s] a mystique of war that only male comrades can comprehend" (30). For instance, Norman Bowker imagines his father, who had his own war, as capable of understanding Norman's experiences in Vietnam.

While I find Smith's article thoughtful and intriguing, and while I agree with much feminist criticism of Vietnam War literature, this essay proposes that the work of Tim O'Brien, particularly *The Things They Carried*, stands apart from the genre as a whole. O'Brien is much more self-consciously aware of gender issues and critical of traditional gender dichotomies than are the bulk of U.S. writers about the Vietnam War. Though it is often tempting to forget it, readers must always bear in mind the distinction between O'Brien-the-narrator and O'Brien-the-author. This difference is crucial to understanding the book's central questions: What is truth and how can truth best be communicated? How can we truly understand the experiences of another human being? I would suggest that O'Brien posits two very different responses to these questions and that his responses are directly related to some of the concerns about gender raised by feminist critics. The male characters in the book do indeed subscribe to patriarchal and condescending attitudes about gender; they believe that knowledge is attained experientially and thus they exclude women from understanding the war experience. Yet, always running counter to this view is its corrective: that trauma is communicable, that understanding may be attained though the imaginative acts of storytelling and reading, and that the male characters do not necessarily understand war and gender as well as they think they do.

I. "The Things They Carried" and "Love"

The book's opening story, "The Things They Carried," offers two competing narratives: the ultra-realistic, precise details of what the men carry (down to brand names and weights of objects listed in ounces) versus the more personal, more traumatic story of the death of Ted Lavender. Such a form underscores one of the novel's main concerns, the relation between fact and fiction—already a troubled question before the first story even begins. While the copyright page makes the usual disclaimers about this being an imaginative work of fiction, the book is dedicated to its characters, as if these are real people, and the epigraph from *John Ransom's Andersonville Diary* asserts the truth of what is to follow. The concrete specificity of the lists in the opening story work along with the book's dedication and epigraph to set readers up to expect a hard-nosed, factual account of the war. Thus, we might mistakenly read Jimmy Cross's story as fact as well—an omniscient, third-person account of the reality of war experience. Such a reading would be a mistake, though. We must remember that the story of Ted Lavender's death is filtered through the subjective experience of Lieutenant Jimmy Cross. It is a narrative that increasingly interrupts and subsumes the more objective story of the items the men carry with them in the field. Yet, it is *not* a story about men at war having to renounce the feminine. Rather, it is about the inevitable guilt associated with war deaths and what soldiers do with that guilt.

While Jimmy Cross certainly views Martha as inhabiting another world, separate from the war, and thus as representing home, purity, an innocence he no longer retains, I'd argue that readers are not supposed to make the same easy gender classifications that Cross does. This point is driven home by Cross's reaction to Lavender's death. Cross is not only a romantic who fantasizes a love affair that's not really there with Martha, he greatly exaggerates his responsibility for Lavender's death. The very randomness of Lavender's death—he is "zapped while zipping," shot after separating from the men briefly to urinate—belies Jimmy Cross's responsibility for the death. Cross blames himself for the death because, as the narrator tells us in a later story, "In the Field," "When a man died, there had to be blame" (177). The soldiers wish to find a reason for the deaths they witness in order to make them less frightening, less random and meaningless. Blame can provide the illusion that war deaths such as those of Lavender and Kiowa are preventable, if only someone behaves differently, more responsibly, in the future. So, Cross determines that his love for Martha, his fantasies about her, are the cause of Lavender's death and that, to prevent such deaths in the future, he will strictly follow standard operating procedures and "dispense with love," focusing instead on duty. Ironically, Lavender dies after the platoon has just finished searching Viet Cong tunnels, a tactic that *was* standard operating procedure, but an extremely dangerous undertaking. While Lee Strunk emerges intact from such a risky assignment, Ted Lavender dies a few moments later completely unexpectedly, while conducting the ordinary business of living.

Again, readers are supposed to see the irrationality of both Cross's burden of guilt as well as his resolve to be a better officer. In fact, it is his very refusal to question orders, to deviate from standard operating procedure, that leads him to camp in the "shitfield" later in the book and inadvertently brings about the death of Kiowa, another accident, and one which many different characters claim blame for. Readers, then, are not supposed to see Cross's burning of Martha's picture and renunciation of the imagination as "sad but necessary" consequences of war, but rather as the attempts of a romantic and guilt-ridden young man to gain control over a situation in which he actually has very little power (Smith, "Things" 24). Because the burning of Martha's picture is linked to the burning of the Vietnamese village, readers see even more fully how mistaken and irrational Cross is in his reaction to Layender's death.

The second story in the collection, "Love," further complicates our view of "The Things They Carried." In "Love," readers are first introduced to the character of narrator Tim O'Brien who remembers Jimmy Cross coming to talk to him at his home years after the war ended. Placed as it is immediately after the opening story and involving two of the same central characters (Martha and Jimmy Cross), "Love" comments on and draws attention to the fictive status of the previous story. In fact, readers discover, at the end of "Love," that the story "The Things They Carried" is written by narrator O'Brien, who explains,

> For the rest of his visit I steered the conversation away from Martha. At the end, though, as we were walking out to his car, I told him that I'd like to write a story about some of this. Jimmy thought it over and then gave me a little smile. "Why not?" he said. "Maybe she'll read it and come begging. There's always hope, right?"
>
> "Right," I said.
>
> He got into his car and rolled down the window. "Make me out to be a good guy, okay? Brave and handsome, all that stuff. Best platoon leader ever." He hesitated for a second. "And do me a favor. Don't mention anything about—"
>
> "No, I said, "I won't." (29)

What about this silence that remains at the end of "Love"? When Cross begs O'Brien, "Don't mention anything about—," what does he mean? Is he referring to the death of Ted Lavender or is he hinting at some other event, one which O'Brien does remain silent about? While Lorrie Smith reads the ambiguity of this ending as indicative of a bond between the two men, who "wordlessly understand each other" (28), it seems to me that the relationship between O'Brien and Cross is more complex. If Cross is referring here to Ted Lavender's death, must we not read O'Brien the narrator as betraying his friend? Even if O'Brien abides by his promise to Cross, repressing something even more troubling than Lavender's death, why the dark hint about some worse secret? Surely this betrays the spirit, if not the letter, of Cross's request. Even more, why include this vignette at all, except to complicate the previous story?

Author O'Brien deliberately juxtaposes these two stories to make readers question the perceptions presented in the previous story. Readers see that the events surrounding Lavender's death are filtered not only through Cross's subjective and guilt-laden impressions, but are then shaped into fiction by the Tim O'Brien character who may or may not be a reliable narrator. The fact that narrator O'Brien tells us about Cross's desire to come off as handsome and brave, the "best platoon leader ever," should deconstruct for readers Cross's macho resolves at the end of "The Things They Carried." Among other things, Cross determines not to fantasize about Martha anymore, to think about her only as belonging elsewhere. A new "hardness" develops in his stomach along with a new firmness to carry out his duties. He resolves to "be a man" about his responsibility for Lavender's death, confessing his culpability to his troops. He determines to love his men more than he loves women, yet to remain strong and distant from them, "leaving no room for argument or discussion" when he issues orders (25). Cross's intent here is to become, in many respects, the traditional American John Wayne–type hero, an icon of American individualism and courage who moves from the western frontier to the "new frontier" of Vietnam. In fact, the story ends with explicit frontier imagery as Jimmy Cross pictures his men "saddling up" and moving "west" under his command in the last line of the story (26). Even if narrator O'Brien is trying to fulfill Cross's request to come off as a stereotypical war hero, author O'Brien exposes the falseness of such constructs by laying bare his own devices.

The story "Love" also should make readers question the portrait of Martha presented in the previous story. In "Love," Martha still seems distant and alone as she was in "The Things They Carried," but she is no longer the dreamy poet of Cross's earlier imaginings. She is a trained nurse and a Lutheran missionary who has seen a great deal of the world, having served in Ethiopia, Guatemala, and Mexico, locales as exotic-sounding as Vietnam probably was to the young, inexperienced Jimmy Cross before his war years. When Cross tells Martha of his strangely violent yet tender college fantasy of tying her to the bed and stroking her knee all night, Martha replies that she can't understand "the things men do" (29). Taken by itself, this moment seems to cement Martha's outsider status; while the narrator and Jimmy Cross understand each other, Martha is cold and unreceptive and only increases Cross's suffering. But the phrase "the things men do," first appears in the previous story, in the mind of Jimmy Cross after he determines to banish Martha from his thoughts:

Henceforth, when he thought about Martha, it would be only to think that she belonged elsewhere. He would shut down the daydreams. This was not Mount Sebastian, it was another world, where there were no pretty poems or midterm exams, a place where men died because of carelessness and gross stupidity. Kiowa was right. Boom-down, and you were dead, never partly dead.

Briefly, in the rain, Lieutenant Cross saw Martha's gray eyes gazing back at him.

He understood.

It was very sad, he thought. The things men carried inside. The things men did or felt they had to do.

He almost nodded at her, but didn't. (24–25)

Martha's disapproval here is clearly a product of Cross's own guilt-ridden imagination. He pictures her "gray eyes gazing back at him" and condemning him silently for shutting her out. Surely the later scene's conscious echoing of the language used earlier should remind us that all of Cross's interactions with Martha are tainted by a masculine anxiety over his failure to be "the best platoon leader ever." Cross projects his anxiety and guilt onto his imaginary, disapproving Martha who cannot understand "the things men do." Yet, author O'Brien painstakingly shows us that the failure to understand another person works both ways. When Martha tells Cross about her life since college—her missionary service and the fact that she never married—O'Brien writes that "it occurred to [Cross] that there were things about her he would never know" (28). While her missionary background in the third world hints at hardship and self-sacrifice perhaps comparable to Cross's war experiences, neither Martha nor Jimmy Cross pursue a more detailed understanding of the other's life. The revised background on Martha should suggest to readers that she, too, had "things to carry," things that Cross cannot know anymore than those who were not in Vietnam can comprehend the war experience.

II. "How to Tell a True War Story"

Perhaps the story in the collection most disturbing to feminist critics is "How to Tell a True War Story." Lorrie Smith argues that this story, as it attempts to build a "deep compassion for the anguish and loss . . . men feel" does so by being "explicitly misogynist" and "ferociously reassert[ing]" traditional notions of manhood ("Things" 29). Smith begins her analysis by examining the character of Rat Kiley and his reaction to the sudden, grotesque death of his friend, Curt Lemon. After Rat writes a long letter to Curt's sister, the narrator informs us, using Rat's own words, that "the dumb cooze never writes back" (O'Brien, *Things* 68). Smith argues that readers are to feel sympathy for Rat because of the suffering he has undergone and to forgive him the violence of his reaction to Curt Lemon's death, as we were earlier to forgive Jimmy Cross, because both are "just boys" and because, as the narrator informs us, true war stories show an "absolute and uncompromising allegiance to obscenity and evil"; thus the offensive word "cooze" is specifically chosen by Rat (*Things* 69). Even more troubling for Smith is her view that the Tim O'Brien narrator steps outside of the story to blame an "implicitly female" reader for refusing to understand male suffering ("Things" 29). Smith argues that the "coda" at the end of the story, when the narrator repeats the word "cooze" in response to an older woman who praises his story about a mutilated baby water buffalo implicates the narrator himself in the misogyny, so that we can no longer excuse it as being mouthed by a "young, hurt, ignorant" soldier who is the "unwitting product of his culture" ("Things" 30). Smith writes, "The sole function of this postscript is to solidify the male bond and ridicule and reject the feminine, which it does with stunning hostility" ("Things" 31).

But it seems to me that a careful reading of the letter Rat writes to Curt's sister shows that author Tim O'Brien deliberately crafts it to highlight certain ironies overlooked by narrator Tim O'Brien who is telling the story. First, Rat uses excessively macho and racist language in the letter, telling Curt's sister that her brother had "stainless steel balls" and that he "liked testing himself, just man against gook. A great, great guy . . ." (67). While narrator O'Brien completely overlooks the irony inherent in the juxtaposition of these last two statements, telling readers simply that "it's a terrific letter," surely author O'Brien wants us to consider how such assertions might affect Curt's sister, who has never met Rat and who lives in a different world entirely, not desensitized to the violence and horror of war as Rat and his buddies are. The letter becomes even more disturbing when Rat continues, writing that Curt made "the war seem almost fun, always raising hell and lighting up villes and bringing smoke to bear every which way" (68). He then tells Curt's sister a specific story which Rat describes as "probably the funniest thing in world history," about Curt going fishing with a crate of hand grenades. "All that gore," Rat writes admiringly, "about twenty zillion dead gook fish. Her brother, he had the right attitude" (68). Rat adds another personal story as well, this one about Curt on Halloween: "the dude paints up his body all different colors and puts on this weird mask and hikes over to a ville and goes trick-or-treating almost stark naked, just boots and balls and an M-16. A tremendous human being . . ." (68). Again, author O'Brien clearly wants readers to notice that what Rat praises in Curt are qualities that would most likely seem frightening and horrific to someone back at home.

Rat concludes his letter by telling the sister that he and Curt were "like soul mates . . . like twins or something, they had a whole lot in common" (68). Then comes the clincher: narrator O'Brien writes, "He tells the guy's sister he'll look her up when the war's over" (68). Author O'Brien carefully places this paragraph to immediately precede the information that the sister never answers Rat's letter. The attentive reader should not be surprised by this news. We are meant to imagine the effect that such a brutal letter would have on Curt's sister. Rat's insistence that he is just like Curt, after having told such disturbing stories about him, and even more, his promise (threat?) to look the sister up after the war, are surely enough to ensure that he'll never hear from her again. Readers are not supposed to simply sympathize with Rat here, but to see past him. Part of the tragedy of these soldiers' experience in Vietnam is that the war has taught them that macho posturing and brutality are the norm. Rat is so immersed in the violence of his experience that he cannot imagine the effect his letter might have on Curt's sister.

But readers of this story are supposed to see past narrator O'Brien as well, who, while obviously thoughtful and intelligent in many ways, is not immune to some of the same blindnesses as the other soldier characters. We've already seen that the narrator does not acknowledge the strange disparities in Rat's letter—that every time Rat praises Curt, it's for some statement or action that seems racist, violent, or grotesque to readers. Narrator O'Brien is subject to the same rage and hatred that many of his characters exhibit; he, too, is damaged by his wartime experiences. And he is not always an admirable character. It is possible that he betrays his friend Jimmy Cross, and he often seems manipulative as he changes or denies stories in mid-stream. In the story "Ghost Soldiers" we see a quite mean-spirited O'Brien who desires revenge for the mistakes of a green, untested medic. The narrator even says about himself: "I'd turned mean inside. Even a little cruel at times. For all my education, all my fine liberal values, I now felt a deep coldness inside me, something dark and beyond reason. It's a hard thing to admit, even to myself, but I was capable of evil" (200).

Thus, when the narrator condemns the older woman at the end of "How to Tell a True War Story" as a "dumb cooze" who doesn't listen, readers should not take this sentiment to express the views of author O'Brien. In interviews, O'Brien has consistently insisted that he should not be confused with the narrator of the book. Speaking with Daniel Bourne and Debra Shostak, O'Brien refers to this particular scene, noting that "there's a simmering anger and resentment on the part of this Tim narrator toward women." He continues,

Remember the Rat Kiley story, where the sister never wrote back, "the dumb cooze," the language used throughout, the reference to the wife lying in bed at night, the "older woman of kindly temperament and humane politics" who "hates war stories" and "all the blood and gore." There's a rage that goes through that story that was entirely intentional, but doesn't represent my own rage necessarily, but the rage that could be the consequence of men doing all the fighting and women being excluded from it. Not a political rage, but a sense of "well, here we are in the war and there they are back home." It's a rage I saw exemplified on a lot of occasions. . . . Exploring these issues is important to me, and even without having the lead characters be women, I can explore this. (88)

Author O'Brien, then, claims that he explores rather than endorses the gender resentment depicted in "How to Tell a True War Story" and elsewhere. Why should we believe him? And what about the addition of that qualifier, "necessarily" after he states that the story doesn't represent his own rage? While I would concede that the end of "How to Tell a True War Story" is particularly off-putting and disturbing to women readers, it also seems to me that the rage represented in the story is mitigated and transformed elsewhere.

Tellingly, the story about Curt Lemon trick-or-treating in the village on Halloween, which Rat includes in his letter to Curt's sister, is retold in "The Lives of the Dead," the book's final story. Narrator O'Brien recounts how, occasionally, "Rat Kiley liked to spice [the story] up with extra details." This time, though, the tale seems even more ominous than the earlier version, as the "extra details" deal directly with gender relations, hinting at a possible rape:

"See, what happens is, it's like four in the morning, and Lemon sneaks into a hootch with that weird ghost mask on. Everybody's asleep, right? So he wakes up this cute little mama-san. Tickles her foot. 'Hey Mama-san,' he goes, real soft like. 'Hey Mama-san—trick or treat!' Should've seen her *face*. About freaks. I mean, there's this buck naked ghost standing there, and he's got this M-16 up against her ear and he whispers, 'Hey, Mama-san, trick or fuckin' treat!' Then he takes off her pj's. Strips her right down. Sticks the pajamas in his sack and tucks her into bed and heads for the next hootch." (239–240)

While narrator O'Brien ostensibly relates this story only to make the point that Curt can seem alive again when stories are told about him, author

O'Brien purposefully expands the earlier story to further highlight the soldiers' misogyny. Rat remains silent about what actually happens to the Vietnamese woman, though he again reiterates praise of Curt Lemon immediately after reciting a chilling story about him: "Lemon—there's one class act," Rat grins and murmurs immediately after the telling. Readers might well wonder what "tuck[ing] her into bed" actually involves—is this Rat's strangely tender euphemism for rape? Sex and violence are explicitly linked in this passage: the M-16 metaphorically suggests a phallus, the "weapon" Curt possibly uses against the Vietnamese woman. (We should remember that, earlier, Rat described Curt as having "stainless steel balls"—in both instances the male body merges with the weaponry of war.) In any case, author O'Brien is doing much more here than simply solidifying traditional male bonds by rejecting the feminine. Why would he include this more detailed information about Curt Lemon's Halloween pranks except to further deconstruct the wartime machismo that Rat and even narrator O'Brien so admire in Curt? After hearing this expanded version of the story, readers would be hard put to continue to blame Curt's sister for not answering Rat's letter. As happens throughout the book, a later story alters or dismantles "truths" presented in an earlier story.

III. "Sweetheart of the Song Tra Bong"

Any analysis of gender in *The Things They Carried* has to grapple with the story in which a woman character figures most prominently: "Sweetheart of the Song Tra Bong." In this story, a young, bored medic named Mark Fossie arranges to bring his seventeen-year-old high school sweetheart, Mary Anne Bell, to the small medical detachment west of Chu Lai, near the village of Tra Bong, where he is stationed. Mary Anne arrives as a fresh-faced all-American girl-next-door type, dressed in culottes and a pink sweater and carrying a plastic cosmetic case. In Vietnam, though, she quickly changes, becoming fascinated not only with the soldiering life, but with the Vietnamese people. She begins to spend time with a group of mysterious Green Berets, even accompanying them when they go out on ambush, and eventually disappearing into the jungle altogether. In a very compelling reading of "Sweetheart," Lorrie Smith argues that Mary Anne Bell is presented as "monstrous" because she "dares to appropriate masculine codes of behavior" ("Things" 32). A woman who defies traditional notions of gender, Mary Anne becomes more horrific, more savage, than any of the male soldiers, thus validating the normalcy of the regular soldiers. While Smith argues that the story is ultimately about "defending men's homosocial bonds against all threat of feminine invasion," O'Brien himself sees the story as underscoring basic similarities between men and women ("Things" 32).

"My feeling," O'Brien says in an interview, "is that what happened to me as a man in Vietnam could happen to a woman as well. And the reasons it didn't were reasons of sociology and demography, not a difference in spirit" (Coffey 61). "Sweetheart" is a story about transgressing boundaries: narrative boundaries, gender boundaries, racial and national boundaries, as well as ethical boundaries. But part of O'Brien's point in the story is that gender and racial divisions, which may seem natural and innate, really operate according to agreed-upon rules. These divisions are social and artificial constructs the same way that guidelines for good storytelling and generic categories such as fact and fiction are.

The story begins by evoking borders, boundaries: the stories about Vietnam that will last forever, the narrator tells us, "are those that swirl back and forth across the border between trivia and bedlam, the mad and the mundane" (89). The first boundary the story upsets is one that O'Brien has worked to undermine throughout the book as a whole: the distinction between truth and fiction. The narrator immediately tells readers that he heard this particular story from Rat Kiley, "who swore up and down to its truth." Yet, among the men in Alpha Company, "Rat had a reputation for exaggeration and overstatement, a compulsion to rev up the facts" (69). So, the veracity of the story is in doubt from the very beginning. But, as he does elsewhere in the book, O'Brien plays with the notion of truth in the first place, the idea that one can easily separate fact from fiction or have access to the simple truth of another's experience. The narrator tells us that most of the men automatically discounted "sixty or seventy percent of anything [Rat] had to say. If Rat told you, for example, that he'd slept with four girls one night, you could figure it was about a girl and a half" (69). Of course, the joke here is that the "truth," derived after subtracting for Rat's exaggeration, is harder to believe than the fiction. It is, in fact, impossible. So, the "truth" becomes simply another story. Author O'Brien, in using this particular example, draws attention to the fact that the soldiers' relationships with women are not based on hard and fast realities, but are largely products of their own imaginings and socialization. And in the beginning of Rat's story about Mark and Mary Anne, gender roles are carried out in accordance with traditional Western stereotypes about men and women. Initially, the men at Chu Lai conceive of women in a conventionally dichotomous way: either as sex objects or as emblems of a kind of innocent domesticity.

Eddie Diamond first suggests bringing women onto the base to serve the men's sexual needs: "What they should do," he suggests, is "pool some bucks and bring in a few mama-sans from Saigon, spice things up . . ." (93). Asian women, in particular, are viewed as sex objects by the American soldiers. Mitchell Sanders, who is listening to Rat tell the story, voices a similar view of women. Rat's story "don't ring true," he says: "I mean, you just can't import your own personal poontang" (90). Sanders speaks for those in the story who obey traditional distinctions. Not only does he talk about women as "poontang," he insists throughout that Rat stick to narrative convention as he tells the story. Even Mark Fossie, who keeps returning to Diamond's suggestion, uses sexualized language when he asserts that bringing a woman to the base could be done: "A pair of solid brass balls, that's all you'd need" (93). When Mary Anne actually arrives at the base, she is described as coming in "by helicopter along with the daily resupply shipment out of Chu Lai" (93). She is simply another supply, whose purpose is to fulfill the men's needs. Yet, Mary Anne, unlike the "mama-sans" suggested by Eddie Diamond earlier, turns out to be an all-American girl. When the men actually see her for the first time, they switch narratives; Mary Anne is transformed from whore to innocent. Rat describes her a "a tall, big-boned blonde . . . seventeen years old, fresh out of Cleveland Heights Senior High. She had long white legs and blue eyes and complexion like strawberry ice cream. Very friendly, too" (93). Later, she is described as a "doll" and as a "cheerleader visiting the opposing team's locker room" (96). We find out that she and Mark Fossie "had been sweethearts since grammar school" who plan to marry and to live "in a fine gingerbread house near Lake Erie, and have three healthy yellow-haired children, and grow old together, and no doubt die in each other's arms and be buried in the same walnut casket" (94).

While Mark and Mary Anne initially try to make their dream work in Vietnam—they "set up house" and stick together "like a pair of high school steadies"—Mary Anne soon begins to transgress her domestic role. She is curious about weaponry; she asks intelligent questions and soon learns to assemble and use an M-16. She helps out in the surgery, seems fascinated by casualties, and is unafraid of getting her hands bloody. She also crosses traditional boundaries separating the American soldiers from their Vietnamese allies. Rat, as he's telling the story, emphasizes a separation between the Vietnamese and American soldiers. He describes the compound at Chu Lai:

> Surrounding the place were tangled rolls of concertina wire, with bunkers and reinforced firing positions at staggered intervals, and base security was provided by a mixed units of RFs, PFs, and ARVN infantry. Which is to say virtually no security at all. As soldiers, the ARVNs were useless; the Ruff-and-Puffs were outright dangerous. (91)

While Rat reiterates American stereotypes of the South Vietnamese soldiers as lazy or cowardly, Mary Anne actually spends time with the ARVNs out along the perimeter, "picking up little phrases of Vietnamese, learning how to cook rice over a can of Sterno, how to eat with her hands" (95–96). She insists upon visiting the village of Tra Bong as well, wanting "to get a feel for how people lived, what the smells and customs were" (96). Again, she behaves quite differently toward the villagers than we've seen American soldiers behaving in previous stories. There is no threat of violence in her visits. We might compare Mary Anne's attitude to that of Curt Lemon and of Rat Kiley himself who praises Curt for "lighting up villes and bringing smoke to bear every which way" in "How to Tell a True War Story" (68).

The demise of Mark and Mary Anne's relationship is foreshadowed when Rat tells us that the bunker the two have chosen as their new home is "along the perimeter, near the Special Forces hootch." The Greenies are also boundary transgressors. Set up along the very edge of the perimeter, they operate in a shadowy, ethically murky world. The Green Berets or Special Forces were first organized as counterinsurgency specialists in the 1950s. Critic John Hellmann claims that the group "became a leading symbol" of President Kennedy's idea of the New Frontier (37). In Kennedy's vision, Hellmann argues, America could revive the virtues of its frontier mentality, spreading liberty to the darker races of Indochina while redeeming itself from the destructive excesses of its earlier westward expansion. The Green Berets, then, served a strange, dual purpose; they were highly trained professional killers with the mission of toppling the Communist government who, at the same time, "engaged in the missionary work of the Peace Corpsman" (Hellmann 47). In "Sweetheart of the Song Tra Bong," the Greenies retain the covert nature of their origins. They "sometimes vanish[ed] for days at a time or even weeks," on their secretive missions, suddenly reappearing "just as magically" (92). None of the medics dare ask questions about their operations; contact between the Greenies and the medics is minimal. O'Brien uses the Green Berets to suggest the tension between America's overt mission in Vietnam—to save the Vietnamese from Communist oppression—and the covert, often grotesque and horrifying methods used. With their savage, animalistic den, their piles of bones, and their sign welcoming visitors to "ASSEMBLE YOUR OWN GOOK!!" the Greenies in the story disrupt the myth of the decent, upright American soldier, much as Mary Anne Bell disrupts myths about traditional womanhood.

As Mary Anne becomes more accustomed to life at Chu Lai, she begins to question the earlier narrative of domestic bliss which she had shared with Mark Fossie: "Not necessarily three kids, she'd say. Not necessarily a house on Lake Erie. 'Naturally we'll still get married,' she'd tell him, 'but it doesn't have to be right away. Maybe travel first. Maybe live together. Just test it out, you know?'" (99). And Mary Anne changes physically as well, in ways that make

Fossie distinctly uncomfortable: "Her body seemed foreign somehow—too stiff in places, too firm where the softness used to be ... Her voice seemed to reorganize itself at a lower pitch" (99). Author O'Brien's repetition of the word "seemed" in this passage draws attention to the fact that we're observing Mary Anne through Mark Fossie's perceptions of her (perceptions which are then reinterpreted by Rat Kiley and finally by narrator O'Brien). When Mary Anne transgresses Fossie's narrow expectations of what a woman should be, he can only imagine her as becoming more like a man. Fossie's discomfort reaches its climax one night when Mary Anne doesn't return to their shared bunker. Rat describes Fossie on the point of collapse: "He squatted down, rocking on his heels, still clutching the flashlight. Just a boy—eighteen years old. Tall and blond. A gifted athlete. A nice kid, too, polite and good-hearted, although for the moment none of it seemed to be serving him well" (100). At this point, the sweethearts have exchanged gender roles. Fossie is described in terms similar to those initially used for Mary Anne—he is young, tall, blond, nice, polite and good-hearted. When the power in the relationship shifts from Mark Fossie to Mary Anne Bell, so do the men's perceptions of their gender attributes.

At first, when Eddie Diamond and Rat go to check on Mark Fossie who has stationed himself outside the Greenies' hootch, they hear only a weird sort of music, with lyrics that "seemed to be in a foreign tongue" (108). Mark insists that the voice is Mary Anne's. When he bursts into the bunker, his suspicions are confirmed. The men find Mary Anne amid a horrific scene—piles of bones and animal skins, lit candles, the smoke of incense, and an appalling, animal stench. The voice that the men could not understand is indeed Mary Anne's. But "the grotesque part," Rat tells us, "was her jewelry. At the girl's throat was a necklace of human tongues" (110). As critic Katherine Kinney points out, the necklace of tongues "testifies to [Mary Anne's] violently earned right to tell war stories" while at the same time showing that she earns this right at the expense of the Vietnamese who "are literally dismembered, figured only as pieces of skin and the tongues Mary Anne has appropriated to voice her own experience" (155, 156). When Mary Anne tells Mark Fossie and Rat Kiley that they're in a place "where [they] don't belong," she means much more than the Greenies' bunker (111). She questions the very presence of Americans in Vietnam. Mary Anne finally speaks in what Rat describes as "a language beyond translation" because she points up the many contradictions and paradoxes of the American experience in Vietnam, both on the home front and in the paddies and jungles of Vietnam (112). American women are supposed to be innocent and pure emblems of home and domesticity, symbols of what will be lost if too many dominoes fall in the Cold War, but Mary Anne is not. American soldiers are supposed to be the good guys, there to save the Vietnamese people from the evils of Communist oppression, but Mary Anne's necklace of tongues signifies otherwise.

O'Brien has reiterated, both in his fiction and in interviews, his belief that war stories are about more than war. In a lecture at Brown University in April of 1999, O'Brien said, "War stories aren't always about war, per se. They aren't about bombs and bullets and military maneuvers. They aren't about tactics, they aren't about foxholes and canteens. War stories, like any good story, are finally about the human heart." "Sweetheart of the Song Tra Bong" works on both a political and a personal level; the story not only exposes the darkness at the heart of the American political and military mission in Vietnam (both Smith and Kinney argue that the story alludes to Conrad's novel), it also explores human relationships on a more individual level. Mary Anne's necklace of tongues suggests her nearly ravenous desire to consume and destroy the other. "I want to *eat* this place," she explains. "Vietnam. I want to swallow the whole country—the dirt, the death—I just want to eat it and have it there inside me. That's how I feel. It's like . . . this appetite" (111). Her desire to know and understand the Vietnamese people has grown into a perverse longing to actually incorporate them into her own body. Surely suggestive of America's desire to create a capitalist Vietnam in its own image while largely ignoring the other country's culture and history, Mary Anne's appetite is reflected in personal relationships presented elsewhere in the novel. Lieutenant Jimmy Cross in "The Things They Carried" is so overwhelmed by his love for Martha that "he wanted to sleep inside her lungs and breathe her blood and be smothered" (11). The narrator in the final story describes his childhood love for Linda in similar terms: "Even then, at nine years old, I wanted to live inside her body. I wanted to melt into her bones—*that* kind of love" (228). These male characters' desire to know and understand the female other is imagined in terms of a literal blending of physical bodies.

This is a theme that O'Brien develops further in his 1994 novel, *In The Lake of the Woods*. A desire to meld completely with another also motivates O'Brien's main character in this book, Senator John Wade. The narrator writes,

> There were times when John Wade wanted to open up Kathy's belly and crawl inside and stay there forever. He wanted to swim through her blood and climb up and down her spine and drink from her ovaries and press his gums against the firm red muscle of her heart. He wanted to suture their lives together. (71)

Wade's love for his wife, Kathy, is so obsessive that it becomes destructive, an urge to actually consume the other person. Although readers never find out definitively what happens to Kathy Wade, the book leaves open the possibility that Wade might actually have murdered his wife in order to possess her completely. Yet, O'Brien seems careful not to present this longing to meld completely with another person as simply a male desire to dominate a feminine other. The male characters in each of the previous examples imagine themselves being incorporated into rather than consuming the female body. Further, the narrator of *In The Lake of the Woods*, in his pursuit to find out the truth surrounding Kathy's disappearance, muses on his own desire to fully understand John Wade: "What drives me on, I realize, is a craving to force entry into another heart, to trick the tumblers of natural law, to perform miracles of knowing. It's human nature. We are fascinated, all of us, by the implacable otherness of others" (101). In order to support his view that gender differences are largely cultural and situational rather than biological and innate, author O'Brien carefully orchestrates parallels between Mary Anne and certain male characters, both in *The Things They Carried* and elsewhere in his writing. Mary Anne Bell is not so different from Jimmy Cross, from nine-year-old Timmy, or from John Wade. She falls prey to the same malady which affects these characters—she wishes to destroy boundaries separating one individual from another, to merge so completely with the other that she herself "burn[s] away into nothing" (111).

Rat's story about Mary Anne Bell stops "almost in midsentence" after his description of her in the Greenies' bunker. Once Mary Anne fully transgresses established social codes—rules codifying not only gender behavior, but racial and national differences, conduct of war, and ethical mores as well—she moves out of the world that Rat Kiley, the medics at Chu Lai, and the soldiers of Alpha Company know and understand and try to cling to despite their chaotic, confusing, and often horrific experiences in Vietnam. Mitchell Sanders' outrage at Rat's pause in his story suggests just such an attempt to adhere to established order:

> Mitchell Sanders stared at him.
> "You can't do that."
> "Do what?"
> "Jesus Christ, it's against the *rules*," Sanders said. "Against human *nature*. This elaborate story, you can't say, Hey, by the way, I don't know the *ending*. I mean, you got certain obligations."
> (112–113)

Sanders' insistence on the rules of proper storytelling is linked to the men's expectations about proper gender conduct. When he says "it's against the rules," he is referring to gender rules as well as narrative rules. Sanders sees both as natural and innate rather than as socially constructed.

Smith argues that the story peters out at this point because "O'Brien cannot imagine an ending for" it ("Things" 36). In her view, Mary Anne exists only to validate traditional gender expectations: "Having appropriated masculine power within a female body," Smith writes, "she is seen as 'dangerous' to the social order" and is thus banished "beyond the periphery of civilization" (36). What Smith fails to point out, however, is that O'Brien does indeed imagine an end for his story; Rat doesn't simply drop the story when Mary Anne eludes his experiential knowledge of women. He turns to his imagination, to "speculation," to provide an ending:

> Rat gave a quick smile. "Patience, man. Up to now, everything I told you is from personal experience, the exact truth, but there's a few other things I heard secondhand. Thirdhand, actually. From here on it gets to be . . . I don't know what the word is."
> "Speculation." (113)

Rat goes on to tell about Mary Anne's love for night patrols, how she takes crazy chances—"things that even the Greenies balked at" (115). Finally, he concludes that Mary Anne "had crossed to the other side," a phrase heavy with implication in this story. Mary Anne has crossed many boundaries: those separating men from women, home front from front line, and "civilized" behavior from savagery. But, in the context of a war story, perhaps the primary suggestion of this phrase is that Mary Anne has indeed switched sides, joined the enemy: the Viet Cong or the North Vietnamese Army. In Rat's ending, Mary Anne is described in terms often used by American soldiers to characterize the Viet Cong: she is shadowy and ghostlike, an unseen but felt presence who seems to be watching the Greenies intently when they go out on ambush. Rat's ending, then, suggests the possibility that Mary Anne has switched political allegiance. A character who refuses to follow rules, to stay where she "belongs," Mary Anne deconstructs American imperialistic tendencies as well as traditional gender imperatives.

Yet, with this ending, O'Brien also makes a point about "the human heart"—the story shows that it is only through imagination that we can ever begin to penetrate what the narrator of *In the Lake of the Woods* calls the "implacable otherness of others." It is exactly Rat's act of imaginative speculation that allows him to proclaim his love for Mary Anne in the end, to move beyond his earlier attitude toward women as "dumb coozes." Thus, when Rat recounts this story to the men after the fact, he too questions established definitions. He disrupts the conventional rules of storytelling with his "tendency to stop now and then, interrupting the flow," his desire "to bracket the full range of meaning," despite Mitchell Sanders' admonishments to "get the hell out of the way and let [the story] tell itself" (106). He also breaks the logic of traditional gender boundaries. Unlike most of the other men, Rat is aware of gender as a socially constructed category. He insists that Mary Anne wasn't dumb, just young: "Like you and me," he argues. "A *girl*, that's the only difference, and I'll tell you something: it didn't amount to jack" (97). And later, Rat argues for the verisimilitude of his story:

> "I know it sounds far-out ... but it's not like *impossible* or anything.... She was a girl, that's all. I mean, if it was a guy, everybody'd say, Hey, no big deal, he got caught up in the Nam shit, he got seduced by the Greenies. See what I mean? You got these blinders on about women. How gentle and peaceful they are. All that crap about how if we had a pussy for president there wouldn't be no more wars. Pure garbage. You got to get rid of that sexist attitude." (106–107)

Author O'Brien surely wants readers to notice the juxtaposition of Rat's own sexist language with his admonition that the men lose their "sexist attitudes." Rat is struggling to overcome his own earlier views, but, like the other men in Alpha Company, he is a product of his society and time.

When these men are presented with a woman who transgresses traditional gender roles, they are uncomfortable, unsure how to react. But they are finally unable to contain her or reincorporate her into the normative world through their stories about her. Mary Anne Bell both *escapes* the limits of their imaginations and expands their notions of what is possible.

IV. "Speaking of Courage" and "Notes"

Norman Bowker in "Speaking of Courage" is another character that readers are supposed to sympathize with, yet see beyond. It's a mistake to read this story as "highly reminiscent of Hemingway's 'Soldier's Home'" in that it presents a woman who willfully refuses to listen to or understand male suffering in wartime (Smith 22). Sally Gustafson in the story is *not* intended to be a real woman; she represents Norman's perceived view of women, his expectations of how they would respond to his war stories. And, as the narrator points out in a sly play on words, Norman "knew shit. It was his specialty" (144). Indeed, O'Brien is careful to emphasize the future subjunctive tense in the scene in which Norman imagines himself speaking to Sally: the phrase "he would have" is repeated numerous times. Perhaps easier to forget is the fact that Norman's dialogue with his father, in which he actually imagines himself talking about his war experiences, also exists only in his imagination. The sympathetic father/listener is as much a created figure as the horrified ex-girlfriend. Like he often does, O'Brien drops hints elsewhere in the book that the truth presented in this story might be suspect. Much earlier, in "Spin," the book's third vignette, we see Norman Bowker talking to the narrator: "I'll tell you something, O'Brien," he says. "If I could have one wish, anything, I'd wish for my dad to write me a letter and say it's okay if I don't win any medals. That's all my old man talks about, nothing else. How he can't wait to see my god-damn medals" (36). In "Speaking of Courage," O'Brien deconstructs the "moments of mutual understanding" which Smith claims male characters in the book are granted (19). Norman's father is not necessarily the kindly, understanding veteran that Norman wishes he were. His friend Max, who Norman also imagines understanding his story—"No doubt Max would've liked it, the irony in particular"—is dead and thus "a pure idea" now (146). Readers are supposed to see that all these characters are "ideas" which exist in Norman's imagination. As he's done earlier, O'Brien uses the next vignette, "Notes," along with several subsequent versions of what happened that night in the "shit field," to comment on and draw attention to the fictive status of "Speaking of Courage."

In "Notes," O'Brien criticizes the first published version of his story about Norman Bowker. "The writing went quickly and easily," he tells us, but "there was a sense of failure. The details of Norman Bowker's story were missing . . . in the end the piece had been ruined by a failure to tell the full and exact truth about our night in the shit field" (159). Yet, over time, O'Brien reports, he forgets the story's flaws and sends a copy to Norman. The narrator then follows abruptly with, "Eight months later [Norman] hanged himself" (160). Norman's death almost seems to result from O'Brien's failure to tell the story properly. Again, O'Brien valorizes the power of the human imagination. While it may be impossible to ever reach the "full and exact truth," it is imperative that we try, that we work diligently to get the story right, that the writing (or the reading, I would add), doesn't simply come "quickly and easily." *The Things They Carried* is intended to be a difficult and often frustrating reading experience for both men and women, precisely because the stakes are so high. O'Brien does not want to suppress or limit the imagination because he believes, finally, that the imagination can save us. The final story in the collection, "The Lives of the Dead," acts as a corrective to the idea posited in the first story, that "imagination was a killer" (11). Just as Rat moves from his hatred of Curt Lemon's sister, the "dumb cooze" who never writes back, to his love for Mary Anne Bell after an act of imaginative speculation, the movement of the book as a whole is to correct Cross's original thinking. By the novel's end, imagination is not a killer but a savior.

V. "The Lives of the Dead"

"The Lives of the Dead" is as much a love story as it is a war story. The book, in fact, could be said to be framed by two love stories—the opening story which tells of Jimmy Cross's love for Martha and the final story which tells of the narrator's love as a nine-year-old for Linda, the little girl who dies of a brain tumor. These love stories add new meaning to what narrator O'Brien tells the kindly older woman who wasn't listening carefully at the end of "How to Tell a True War Story": "It *wasn't* a war story. It was a *love* story," O'Brien tells us (85). While readers may be tempted to read this explanation as a comment about the love of comrades-in-arms, of soldiers for their departed colleagues, by the end, the book opens out to encompass a world larger than that inhabited solely by soldiers. O'Brien's statement about his story becomes an admonishment to all readers who fail to see connections between war experience and larger, more general life experiences. In "The Lives of the Dead," O'Brien deliberately juxtaposes traumatic war deaths with the traumatic death of Linda in order to undermine the old cliché of Vietnam War fiction: "if you weren't there, you can't possibly understand." "The Lives of the Dead" argues for the power of fiction, of imaginative creation. In stories, the dead *can* come to life; experiences *can* be communicated imaginatively.

The powerful status of fiction is perhaps nowhere so well illustrated as in the plot of the movie that nine-year-old Timmy attends on his date with Linda: *The Man Who Never Was*. In the film, the Allies plant false documents on the body of a dead British soldier to mislead the Germans about the site of the upcoming landings in Europe. "The Germans find the documents," O'Brien writes, and "the deception wins the war" (232). The dead soldier's fictional identity is more influential than his actual, biographical identity, which we never discover. In many ways, narrator O'Brien in the book is "the man who never was." He is a created persona whose stories teach us about the difficulty of getting to the truth of individual identity. The narrator looks at a photograph of himself from 1956, realizing that, "in the important ways" he has not changed at all: "the essence remains the same . . . the human life is all one thing, like a blade tracing loops on ice" (236). What shapes a person, then, is difficult to unravel. An individual seems to be the product of biological predisposition as well as a jumble of experiences: wartime experience as well as larger life experience. In any case, human essence and selfhood remain mysterious.

Because O'Brien works so diligently to connect war experience to human experience in general, I do not read his work as excluding or silencing women. One of O'Brien's most moving pieces is a personal essay he published in the *New York Times Magazine* in 1994, called "The Vietnam in Me." In this essay, O'Brien tells two stories simultaneously—the tale of his return to Vietnam over twenty years after having been a soldier there and the story of the disintegration of a serious love relationship. Nearly suicidal over the break-up, O'Brien has difficulty sleeping and writes that he is on "war time, which is the time we're all on at one point or another: when fathers die, when husbands ask for divorce, when women you love are fast asleep beside men you wish were you" (55). Just as in "The Lives of the Dead" O'Brien links the physical corpse of the old Vietnamese man to those of Ted Lavender, Curt Lemon, and Kiowa, and finally to Linda's, O'Brien links wartime experience and life experience in this article. "If there's a lesson in this," he writes, "which there is not, it's very simple. You don't have to be in Nam to be in Nam" (55). While much Vietnam War literature expresses the "incommunicability" of war trauma, which is eased for men because of a shared patriarchal language, O'Brien's work expresses the exact opposite: that through imaginative acts of storytelling and reading, the atrocity of war can begin to be understood and thus can begin to heal.

WORKS CITED

Bonn, Maria. "The Lust of the Eye: Michael Herr, Gloria Emerson and the Art of Observation." *Papers on Language and Literature* 29.1 (Winter 1993): 28–48.

Bourne, Daniel and Debra Shostak. "A Conversation with Tim O'Brien." *Artful Dodge* 17 (1991): 74–90.

Broyles Jr., William. "Why Men Love War." *Esquire* (November 1984): 55–65.

Coffey, Michael. "Tim O'Brien: Inventing a New Form Helps the Author Talk About War, Memory, and Storytelling." *Publishers Weekly* 16 February 1990: 60–61.

Hellmann, John. *American Myth and the Legacy of Vietnam.* New York: Columbia UP, 1986.

Jeffords, Susan. *The Remasculinization of America: Gender and the Vietnam War.* Bloomington: Indiana UP, 1989.

Kinney, Katherine. *Friendly Fire: American Images of the Vietnam War.* Oxford (England); New York: Oxford UP, 2000.

Lawson, Jacqueline. Introduction. *Vietnam Generation Special Issue. Gender and the War: Men, Women, and Vietnam* 1.3–4 (Summer–Fall 1989): 6–11.

O'Brien, Tim. *In the Lake of the Woods.* New York: Houghton Mifflin, 1994.

———. *The Things They Carried.* New York: Houghton Mifflin, 1990.

———. Transcript of President's Lecture. Brown University, Providence, R.I. 21 April 1999. <http://www.stg.brown.edu/projects/WritingVietnam/obrien.html>.

———. "The Vietnam in Me." *New York Times Magazine* 2 October 1994: 48–57.

Smith, Lorrie N. "Back Against the Wall: Anti-Feminist Backlash in Vietnam War Literature. *Vietnam Generation Special Issue. Gender and the War: Men, Women, and Vietnam* 1.3–4 (Summer–Fall 1989): 115–126.

———. "'The Things Men Do': The Gendered Subtext in Tim O'Brien's *Esquire* Stories." *Critique: Studies in Contemporary Fiction* 36.1 (Fall 1994): 16–40.

ALEX VERNON

Salvation, Storytelling, and Pilgrimage in Tim O'Brien's The Things They Carried

Tim O'Brien's *The Things They Carried* participates in a tradition of literary revision unique to twentieth-century American war literature, joining e.e. cummings's World War I novel *The Enormous Room* and Kurt Vonnegut Jr.'s World War II novel *Slaughterhouse-Five* in their evocation of John Bunyan's seventeenth-century spiritual tract *The Pilgrim's Progress* as a mechanism for questioning the possibility of spiritual gain through waging modern war.

The three novels share other characteristics. All three purposefully and explicitly blur the distinctions among author, narrator, and protagonist, and between fact and fiction. Cummings's and O'Brien's first-person narrator-characters bear their authors' names, Edward E. Cummings and Tim O'Brien. We never learn the name of Vonnegut's first-person fictional narrator, but certain facts of his biography, like O'Brien's narrator-character's, match his creator's. Early in O'Brien's text, Tim the narrator receives a visit to his home from Jimmy Cross; early in Vonnegut's text, the narrator visits the home of his old war buddy, Bernard V. O'Hare. And the first lines of *Slaughterhouse-Five* sound very much like something out of *The Things They Carried*: "All of this happened, more or less. The war parts, anyway, are pretty much true" (1). The first American edition of *The Enormous Room* begins with an introduction by cummings's father composed of explanatory narrative and two actual letters

From *Mosaic* 36, no. 4 (December 2003): 171–88. Copyright © 2003 by *Mosaic*.

he had written, to President Woodrow Wilson and to a staff officer from the Judge Advocate General's office in Paris, concerning the imprisonment and release of his son, who of course has the name of both the text's author and its first-person narrator. All three novels also tell their stories recursively, more-or-less following a storyline but doing so in a non-continuous, episodic, and fragmented manner.

The three novels also, given their evocation of *The Pilgrim's Progress*, concern themselves with the subject of salvation. In *The Enormous Room*, within the context of the Bunyan text, cummings writes about salvation in terms of happiness: "To leave [. . .] [the prison] with the knowledge, and worse than that the feeling, that some of the finest people in the world are doomed to remain prisoners thereof for no one knows how long—are doomed to continue, possibly for years and tens of years and all the years which terribly are between them and their deaths, the grey and indivisible Non-existence which without apology you are quitting for Reality—cannot by any stretch of the imagination be conceived as constituting a Happy Ending to a great and personal adventure" (238). The narrator was, he tells us, "happier" in prison "than the very keenest words can pretend to express" (238). Yet in prison he still possessed the same knowledge that precludes happiness, and his declarations while in prison—written when cummings was out of prison—of his happiness and mastery of his own life must be read as tongue-in-cheek. The novel's dominant tone is sarcasm; its historical context is a cultural ideology portraying war as a path for cultures and individuals to attain spiritual progress. Cummings's ideal contemporaneous reader, upon finishing the text, would not by any stretch of the imagination seriously have felt that anything redemptive had occurred or might occur in this all-too-human world.

In 1969, Vonnegut's *Slaughterhouse-Five* invoked *The Pilgrim's Progress* to forever obliterate the idea of attaining any spiritual grace through the absurd inhumanity of modern warfare. It is hard to imagine a more nihilistic note in war fiction than the novel's final "word," the bird call that, like divine judgement, hangs in the air after the firebombing of Dresden, the question itself (much less the nonexistent answer) beyond human articulation: "*Po-tee-wheet?*" (215).

The Things They Carried does not even bother to ask after the possibility of spiritual progress through war. The story "Church" is the book's comic vignette on the conjoining of the spiritual and the martial in the American war in Vietnam. The unit on extended patrol has set up for the night in a church, and, in a perverse moment of reverence, "the older monk carried in a cane chair for the use of Lieutenant Jimmy Cross, placing it near the altar area, bowing and gesturing for him to sit down" (*Things* 120). Jimmy Cross, the military leader with the telling initials and last name, is here nicely juxtaposed against the real cross that O'Brien neglects to mention but that must be near the altar too. "The old monk seemed proud of the chair, and proud that such a man as Lieutenant Cross should be sitting in it." The two monks take "a special liking for Henry Dobbins" (120), the man who ritually wore his girlfriend's pantyhose to make him invulnerable. They call him "good soldier Jesus" (120). They clean and oil his machine gun. Dobbins relates his religious feelings to Kiowa. He believes in God but has never cared for "the religious part" or the intellectual part. For him, what matters is "just being nice to people" (121), and maybe someday he will "find a monastery some-where" and "wear a robe and be nice to people. [. . .] All you can do is be nice. Treat them decent, you know?" (123). The moment for spiritual reckoning passes. In the morning the unit moves out, their bodies bathed in the church water and fed from the church garden, their guns cleaned by monks, their newly vitalized selves ready to waste gooks once again.

Instead, O'Brien asks a different question, perhaps every war writer's essential question: Can one achieve moral or spiritual redemption through storytelling? In this essay, I hope to provide O'Brien's answer to the question. The connections with cummings's and Vonnegut's novels are significant and informing, but my chief concern is with O'Brien's novel and the question it poses. Because *The Things They Carried* never directly alludes to *The Pilgrim's Progress* or otherwise discusses spiritual matters, in the first part of the essay, I attempt to establish the text as a quest for salvation and redemption through the narrator-character's composing process. And, because the essay speculates on the novel as a form of religious pilgrimage, it next turns to Victor Turner's anthropological studies of pilgrimage to explore what Turner might reveal about O'Brien's text. The essay concludes by returning to the initial ques-tion: Can we revisit our wars in writing stories—can we make imaginative pilgrimages back in time and space—and find some solace, some meaning, some salvation?

* * *

The Things They Carried repeatedly attests to the power of storytelling to transform events and to affirm a new kind of truth, one more spiritual than factual, while somehow in the process redeeming us and resurrecting the dead. Such language comes most strongly in the "The Lives of the Dead," the book's final story. "But this too is true," O'Brien's story begins. "Stories can save us. [. . .] In a story, which is a kind of dreaming, the dead some-times smile and sit up and return to the world" (225). O'Brien's narrator Tim recalls conversations he had as a child with a dead friend, the nine-year-old Linda. He recalls a movie they had seen, *The Man Who Never Was*, about a corpse used by the Allies in World War II for delivering false operational plans to deceive the Germans and win the war; about, in other words, a dead man whose death and figurative resurrection saved the world from the evils of Nazi Germany. He recalls the stories told and retold about the dead soldiers from Vietnam, stories always slightly different with each telling, often elaborated beyond the limits of factual, earthly truth, yet true to the spirit of using language to keep the dead alive. "But in a story," Tim the narrator writes, "which is a kind of dreaming, the dead sometimes smile and sit up and return to the world" (225). Such he calls a "miracle" (236), and Tim tells these stories "trying to save Timmy's life with a story" (246)—trying to save the child that he was, his pre-adult, innocent, prelapsarian self.

The message O'Brien imparts is one we have heard before. By faithfully retelling the story of Christ in its several variations, by allowing themselves to believe against all fact in his death and resurrection, Christians animate him and in the process save their prelapsarian souls. His, the maxim goes, is the greatest story ever told. O'Brien seems to want us to read *The Things They Carried* as a literary analogue of the New Testament. The infantry platoon is led by the lieutenant, with the significant last name and initials. With stories commenting on each other and confusing the facts while achieving a greater truth, with two stories ("Spin" and "How to Tell a True War Story") composed of Psalm-like fragments, the book's episodic structure does not wander far from the structural spirit of the Bible—a structure that Maggie Dunn and Ann Morris, in their study of the composite novel, call "the sacred composite" (qtd. in O'Gorman 303). And, despite O'Brien's attestations in "How to Tell a True War Story" that war stories have no morals, *The Things They Carried* offers a number of them, primarily the conspicuous moral of the stories surrounding Kiowa's death: that every citizen, even the old man in Omaha who didn't vote, is responsible for the war and for everything in the war, from Kiowa's death to My Lai.

The opening and title story in *The Things They Carried* details the burdens, physical and emotional, carried by infantrymen in Vietnam. By immediately inviting the reader to join the characters in this journey, a journey that has moral dimensions and the potential for spiritual salvation, *The Things They Carried* echoes Bunyan's *The Pilgrim's Progress*. The very title of O'Brien's book and lead story strongly suggests the burden carried by Bunyan's Christian; indeed, this may be the reason O'Brien selected this story as lead and title instead of, say, "How to Tell a True War Story." Paul Fussell, whose *The Great War and Modern Memory* is a seminal work of literary and cultural criticism on the war, writes of a reference to Bunyan by a World War I British *Daily Express* columnist, that the troops overseas "who had named one of the support trenches of the Hohenzollern Redout 'Pilgrim's Progress,' [. . .] would not fail to notice the similarity between a fully loaded soldier, marching to and from the line with haversack, ground-sheet, blanket, rifle, and ammunition, and the image of Christian at the outset of his adventures" (138). Likewise do O'Brien's soldiers at the very outset of their narrative adventure hump can openers, pocket knives, heat tabs, C rations, water, steel helmets, boots, extra socks, flak jackets, bandages, ponchos, poncho liners, mosquito netting, machetes, and arms and ammunition.

Fussell traces a number of references and similarities in Great War British memoirs to Bunyan's parable and other less popular romance quests: the carried burdens, the ghostliness of the experience, the "action of moving physically through some terrible topographical nightmare" (142), and the incalculable allusions to Bunyan's Slough of Despond and his Valley of the Shadow of Death, all of which O'Brien's book recreates, with twists. In this collection of stories patched together from previously published and new pieces, Christian isn't just the aptly named Jimmy Cross. He is also, and perhaps more directly, Tim, on his narrative quest for salvation. The Slough of Despond, in which Christian finds himself mired in muck, becomes O'Brien's shit field. If the character Help provides the helping hand that pulls Christian from the muck, Norman Bowker (or Tim the narrator?) fails to reach his hand out to save Kiowa—who always carries a New Testament and "had been raised to believe in the promise of salvation under Jesus Christ" (164)—from the sucking field of mud and shit. The disparate fates of Christian and Kiowa aside, Bunyan's and O'Brien's messages are startlingly similar: we are all responsible to one another, we are in this all-too-earthly life together. The ambiguity of whose actions led to Kiowa's death, and who failed to pull him out of the shit field, underscores the fact that one person is not to blame. All are responsible.

Even the three stages of Christian's experience in Bunyan—The Manner of his Setting Out, His Dangerous Journey, and Safe Arrival at the Desired Country—work their way into O'Brien's structure, which, though less linear, includes descriptions of Tim's pre-war self and the manner of his submission to the war, his war-time journey, and his post-war self's arrival home. That the fragmented and recursive nature of *The Things They Carried* has the linearity implied by a journey motif might not accord with many readers' experience of reading the novel, as the novel certainly flirts with the suicidal repetition of Norman Bowker's self-destructive, Dantesque circling of the lake and his own veteran soul in "Speaking of Courage." Indeed, we can read the success of O'Brien's writing career through *The Things They Carried* and the 1994 novel *In the Lake of the Woods* and the essay "The Vietnam in Me" (also 1994), as an extended flirtation with this very dangerous, seductive world of his own memory. Depression and thoughts of suicide plague the author in the essay "The Vietnam in Me," published after his first (and only) return trip to

Vietnam twenty-five years later, after his tour of duty there while, at the end of *In the Lake of the Woods*, the shades of Vietnam in John Wade's life create the situation that amounts to a kind of suicide when he is driven to get in his boat and motor out of the text and out of society permanently. Norman Bowker and his story very much belong to Tim O'Brien and his own narrative. Thus the question of whether the narrative journey in *The Things They Carried* delivers us—delivers Tim—to a place analogous to Christian's Celestial City (as Fussell finds World War I memoirs attempting to do) persists. The novel's recursive form signifies its status not as war story at all but as a post-war story of a veteran struggling with his demons.

I do not mean to suggest that O'Brien or Tim actually hopes to resurrect the dead or save lives destroyed by the war. The text's language of saving lives works metaphorically. Tim the narrator-character returns to war in his fiction desperately seeking some positive meaning in his and his comrades' experiences. He wants to discover a way to alleviate his guilt and burden such that he can return to the war in his memory, emotionally survive the trip, and perhaps even gain from it. It had to mean something, didn't it? For all that suffering? He hopes to recover a little of his pre-war innocence, his faith in himself, everyone else, and the future. He tries to create a religion of writing fiction as a means of transcending the horrible "happening truth" of war. Even if writing affords only fleeting moments of transcendence, perhaps those moments can suffice to carry the soul along. The war itself offered him nothing but darkness; maybe, in writing about it, he can find a ray of light.

Writing for Tim the narrator thus becomes a ritual act, experienced as a dream state. Much of O'Brien's own aesthetic, in this novel and even more manifestly in *Going after Cacciato*, renders the narrator as in a dream state. Milton J. Bates finds *Going after Cacciato* more akin to "the medieval dream-vision" than "either naturalism or 'magical realism'" (275 n.7), more akin to a work like Bunyan's. *The Things They Carried* is a dreamscape novel in its composition process and in Tim the character-narrator's mimicking of O'Brien the author's composition process. O'Brien's writing process is "a mixture of the subconscious and the directed [...]: I'm half living in a rational world and half living in a kind of trance, imagining" (Naparsteck 11). Tim the character-narrator submits himself to the same process in *The Things They Carried*, as he describes one of his conversations with the dead Linda: "It was a kind of self-hypnosis. Partly willpower, partly faith, which is how stories arrive" (244).

O'Brien's 1991 essay "The Magic Show" on the art of storytelling, published only a year after *The Things They Carried*, connects this writing trance to the spiritual state in which the religious shaman operates, "watching the spirits beyond" (178). The essay also explicitly connects O'Brien's artistic credo with the essential Christian one. The piece begins with a memory of his childhood hobby, magic. Its hold on him came from the sense of "the abiding mystery at its heart. Mystery everywhere—permeating mystery—even in the most ordinary objects of the world." Through magic he could imagine a universe "both infinite and inexplicable" where "anything was possible," where "the old rules were no longer binding," where, if he could restore an apparently cleaved necktie, he ought to be able to use his "wand to wake up the dead" (176). O'Brien then reminds us of the dual role in many cultures of magician and storyteller performed by the same person, most commonly in a religious context. In Christianity, Jesus functions as storyteller, miracle worker, and revealer of truth, as O'Brien the writer ideally functions (177–79).

The Things They Carried assigns this shamanistic role to Tim the narrator, who has preserved his childhood sweetheart Linda "in the spell of memory and imagination" in the same way he has preserved the soldiers he knew who died in Vietnam, and in the same way O'Brien writes, and for the same reasons: to happen onto epiphany or understanding or enlightenment; to transcend the ordinary and the actual, to work miracles, to find spiritual relief. Thus the actual Chip becomes the novel's Curt Lemon, whose death Tim reinvents for his own peace of mind.

> Twenty years later, I can still see the sunlight on Lemon's face. I can see him turning, looking back at Rat Kiley, then he laughed and took that curious half step from shade into sunlight, his face suddenly brown and shining, and when his foot touched down, in that instant, he must've thought it was the sunlight that was killing him. It was not the sunlight. It was a rigged 105 round. But if I could ever get the story right, how the sun seemed to gather around him and pick him up and lift him high into a tree, if I could somehow recreate the fatal whiteness of that light, the quick glare, the obvious cause and effect, then you would believe that the last thing Curt Lemon believed, which for him must've been the final truth. (84)

In "The Lives of the Dead," the book's final story, Timmy, while dreaming, talks to the dead Linda, and in this same spirit of dreaming he reanimates his dead buddies. My point is that, to read it as a journey or pilgrimage, we must read *The Things They Carried* not as a war story but as a post-war story, the story of the writer at his desk, not the soldier in the jungle, his childhood wand a pencil now, on an entirely different kind of journey. Indeed, O'Brien omitted the story "Speaking of Courage" from *Going after Cacciato*—the story initially featured *Going after Cacciato*'s Paul Berlin instead of Norman Bowker—because "*Cacciato* was a war story" but "Speaking of Courage" was "a postwar story" (Naparsteck 7), and so belongs in the post-war book *The Things They Carried*.

* * *

Viewing O'Brien's *The Things They Carried* in relation to Bunyan's *The Pilgrim's Progress*, O'Brien's declared faith in the transcendent power of storytelling, and the trancelike state of its composition, suggests another interpretive perspective. Victor Turner's anthropological study of religious pilgrimage—found chiefly in "Pilgrimages as Social Processes" and *Image and Pilgrimage in Christian Culture* (with Edith Turner)—combines Arnold Van Gennep's theory about the liminality of initiatory *rites de passage* with his own theory of spiritual *communitas*, of group member identification through an understanding of an essential sameness and universality. The United States military circumstances of combat in Vietnam conform closely enough to Turner's and Van Gennep's structural models to afford O'Brien a convenient juxtaposition of his military journey's absence of a spiritual component and his writing journey's quest for one.

The first major connection between Van Gennep and the military experience, for the purpose of cultural and literary studies, is Eric J. Leed's *No Man's Land: Combat and Identity in World War I*. According to Leed, the soldier going to war "undergoes rituals of passage, the rites described initially by Arnold Van Gennep. Van Gennep divided rites of passage into three phases: rites of separation, which remove the individual or group of individuals from his or their accustomed place; liminal rites, which symbolically fix the character of the 'passenger' as one who is between states, places, or conditions; and finally rites of incorporation (postliminal rites), which welcome the individual back into the [social] group" (14). Religious pilgrimages and Van Gennep's rites of passage also share geographic liminality. "In many tribal societies" Turner and Turner write, "initiands are secluded in a sacralized enclosure, or *temenos*, clearly set apart from the villages, markets, pastures, and gardens of everyday usage and trafficking." Most Christian ceremonies take place in churches and cathedrals, which are often located in the centre of a town, hardly far from daily life. But pilgrims achieve this liminality by travelling "to a sacred site or holy shrine located at some distance from the pilgrim's place of residence and daily labor" (4). For initiands and pilgrims, this physical movement to the social periphery removes them from daily concerns, responsibilities, obligations, and relationships, freeing them to experience inner spiritual happenings. Daily social life's complicated web of relational identity is radically transformed and simplified so that the individual can discover or assert a more autonomous or purified self, can deal with the journey on his or her own terms.

American soldiers deployed overseas to combat very much escape normal social bonds; they journey, as it were, to the periphery. Turner notes that "the Pali form of the Sanskrit word for pilgrimage" literally means "'retirement from the world'" (182), which nicely contrasts with the phrase that United States soldiers in Vietnam used to refer to the States: *back in the world.* Yet few if any would argue that the United States went to and fought in Vietnam for spiritual reasons. On the other hand, O'Brien's narrative journey to Vietnam, his writing process, and that of Tim the character-narrator do suggest that a pilgrimage is under way. If "pilgrimage is exteriorized mysticism," Turner and Turner write, "mysticism is an interior pilgrimage" (7). The daydreaming trance that brings Linda back to life in "The Lives of the Dead"; the daydreaming trance that O'Brien describes as his writing process and that attempts to create a kind of life after death (in fiction) for his characters, his friends, and himself; the moral accounting that seems to have sent O'Brien the author and Tim the narrator-character to the writing desk in the first place; and the very mystic language he uses to describe his artistic vision in "The Magic Show" all reveal the extent to which writing in general and writing *The Things They Carried* in particular are, for author and narrator-character, an interior pilgrimage. Leed further asserts that returned veterans continue to linger in a liminal zone (194). As Farrell O'Gorman has argued, in *The Things They Carried*, Vietnam is "a region of the psyche rather than of Southeast Asia" (295); or, as O'Brien himself has written, "you don't have to be in Nam to be in Nam" ("Vietnam" 55). His personal moral struggle over his participation in the war sends him back again and again.

One of Turner's most interesting and complex observations about religious pilgrimage concerns its volitional nature. In "Pilgrimages as Social Processes" he first notes how "in ancient Judea, and in modern Islam," the pilgrimage obligation did not apply to everyone. Moreover, "even for those on whom obligation rested[,] the obligation was a moral one; there were no sanctions behind it" because it obtains significance only when "voluntarily undertaken," when it is "regarded as desirable" (174). In other words, because the purpose of pilgrimage is to effect an internal spiritual transformation, one can't just go through the motions. Christian pilgrimage, on the other hand, "tended at first to stress the voluntary aspect and to consider sacred travel to Palestine or Rome as acts of supererogatory devotion"; yet, as the Church intervened to assert some control over what had initially been a tradition outside official structure, "a strong element of obligation came in with the organization of the penitential systems" whereby "pilgrimages were set down as adequate [and authorized] punishments [and penance] for certain crimes." Thus pilgrimages that begin as obligatory obtain a strong element of volition and vice-versa, an apparently inevitable ambiguity reflecting "the liminality of the pilgrimage situation itself" (175) more generally, as simultaneously an act of social duty and individual agency, a social event and an individual experience. Turner concludes that, in pilgrimage,

> we see clearly displayed this tension and ambiguity between status and contract and an attempt to reconcile them in the notion that it is meritorious to *choose one's duty*. Enough room is left to the individual to distance himself briefly from inherited social constraint and duty, but only enough room so as to constitute, as it were, a public platform in which he must make by word or deed a formal public acknowledgement of allegiance to the overarching religious, political, and economic orders. Yet even here appears the thin edge of the contractual wedge that will lead eventually to a major loosening up of the structure of society. Pilgrimages represent, so to speak, an amplified symbol of the dilemma of choice versus obligation in the midst of a social order where status prevails. (177, emph. Turner's)

Viewing pilgrimage as "an amplified symbol of the dilemma of choice versus obligation" brings us to O'Brien and his own decisions, first to go to Vietnam and then to write about it (and write about it and write about it). O'Brien the author and Tim the narrator-character of *The Things They Carried* could have avoided combat duty in Vietnam but ultimately chose to go, as his memoir's epigraph from Dante's *Paradiso* underscores: "[T]he greatest gift that God in his bounty / made in creation . . . / . . . was the freedom of the will" (qtd. in Heberle 58).

That the epigraph from O'Brien's first book, his war memoir *If I Die in a Combat Zone, Box Me Up and Ship Me Home*, comes from Dante's *Paradiso* also suggests the spiritual salvation motivating this embarking moment of his writing career. O'Brien voluntarily returns to Vietnam in his writing to perform an interior pilgrimage. Unlike initiation rites of passage, pilgrimages are repeatable, and while most pilgrims undergo only one in a lifetime—the way most war memoirs are the only book written by the veteran—O'Brien the novelist seems to be a professional pilgrim. For Christian pilgrims, Turner and Turner write, "the mystery of choice resides in the individual" because what matters "is the inward movement of the heart" and "the moral unit is the individual" with the "goal of salvation" (8). Pilgrims go to resolve guilt, to hazard dangers, and pay proper penance for their sins. Pilgrimages represent both the path to miracles and the path through purgatory. They provide coherence, meaning, and direction.

Mark Heberle's study of Tim O'Brien as a "trauma artist" cites Kalí Tal's three criteria for trauma literature: "the experience of trauma, the urge to bear witness, and a sense of community" (qtd. in Heberle 16). The first two elements clearly obtain in O'Brien's texts; the last item, the sense of community, significantly connects with the Turner and Turner pilgrimage model. Turner characterizes the pilgrim group as forming a *normative communitas*, which is a group that is bound by a kind of social contract and that has, as its primary goal, the maintenance, by way of social structure, of the possibility of the group's achieving a spirit of universal fellowship. Pilgrims ideally experience a suspension of social casting "in bonding together, however transiently, at a certain level of social life, large numbers [. . .] who would otherwise never have come into contact" (178) in a manner that again encourages the spirit of *communitas*, which "presses always to universality and ever greater unity" (179). Turner quotes Malcolm X's reflection on his pilgrimage to Mecca and how it fostered in him the "*reality* of the Oneness of Man" beyond colour or other differences (169, emph. Turner's).

The sense of community involved in trauma literature as a condition of healing and the *communitas* sought by pilgrims as a fundamental condition of spiritual development come together in O'Brien the author's and Tim the narrator-character's narrative quests for spiritual healing. *The Things They Carried* constantly reinforces the universalizing spirit engendered by sharing the combat experience and by achieving identification not only with the members of one's unit but also with the enemy and with the reader, even—and especially—those with no military or war experience whatsoever.

The major episode of universalizing identification to the enemy revolves around the man whom Tim the narrator did or didn't kill in "The Man I Killed," "Ambush," and "Good Form." In these stories, Tim the narrator-character identifies with the dead Viet Cong soldier, a man who as he imagines "had been born, maybe, in 1946," the same year as both character-narrator and author. All three come from farm country. The Vietnamese soldier "from his earliest boyhood [. . .] would have listened to stories about the heroic Trung sisters and Tran Hung Dao's famous rout of the Mongols and Le Loi's final victory against the Chinese at Tot Dong," just as Tim O'Brien spent his boyhood listening to tales of World War II from his parents' generation and World War I from his grandparents'. Publicly a supporter of the cause, the man whom Tim did or didn't kill was secretly frightened: "He was not a fighter. [. . .] He liked books. [. . .] At night, lying on his mat, he could not picture himself doing the brave things his father had done, or his uncles, or the heroes of the stories. He hoped in his heart that he would never be tested. He hoped the Americans would go away. Soon, he hoped. He kept hoping and hoping, always, even when he was asleep" (*Things* 125). All of which describe Tim the narrator-character (and O'Brien the author).

O'Brien's language also feminizes the corpse, as its "eyebrows were thin and arched like a woman's," and as the narrator imagines the soldiers as a youth he sees "at school the boys sometimes teased him about how pretty he was, the arched eyebrows and long shapely fingers, and on the playground they mimicked a woman's walk and made fun of his smooth skin" (*Things* 127). Read in the context of the rest of Tim's identification, this passage suggests that Tim sees himself, too, as slender and womanly, that he is recalling a boyhood fraught with such teasing. This feminization of the corpse helps dichotomize the young man's war-fearing sensitive nature from the masculine business of war-making. It also symbolizes the emasculating quality of war, that which renders soldiers passive and powerless; and, rightly or wrongly, readers associate passivity with the feminine. And, if we also accept the conventional thinking (again rightly or wrongly) described by Paul John Eakin in *How Our Lives Become Stories: Making Selves* whereby we understand women to define themselves relationally and men to define themselves autonomously, the feminized corpse embodies the narrator's act of relational, "feminine" identification with another person. We never discover whether Tim the narrator killed the man. If he did, then the survivor's guilt he expresses in these stories further reflects a *communitas* spirit extending beyond his fellow United States soldiers, beyond military, national, racial, and even gender distinctions. If he did not kill the man, then the narrator's imaginative act of killing him and rendering him the narrator's own *Doppelgänger* signifies O'Brien's writing aesthetic of using fiction to achieve moments of identification. Every time Tim recounts or re-imagines the death of a fellow soldier, he plays this identification game. His linking in the book's final story of the little girl Linda, his childhood friend who died when she was nine, with his fellow soldiers who died in Vietnam, reinforces the "feminized" position of the soldier.

O'Brien even takes pains, as all trauma artists do, to communicate his trauma's incommunicability. Why else, finally, would he write about the war if he found it fundamentally incommunicable? Several incidents in *The Things They Carried* reveal moments when the male soldiers cannot communicate with one another, such as Mitchell Sanders's story in "How to Tell a True War Story" about the patrol that heads into the mountains on a listening-post mission and whose bizarre, hallucinatory experience they refuse to tell their colonel when they get back—refuse to tell him, the reader senses, because it cannot be communicated. Later in the book, Tim the narrator finds himself assigned to a desk job at battalion headquarters, away from his line unit, out of the jungle, and such an assignment makes him feel "like a civilian" (*Things* 194). When his old buddies return from a mission, he can no longer connect with them: "They were soldiers," he bemoans; "I wasn't" (198). Paradoxically, this separation from his former comrades creates a *communitas* identification with the reader as O'Brien here connects his narrator's alienation with that of his reader: civilian or veteran, man or woman.

The final instance of connecting the soldier's life with the civilian's appears in the last story of *The Things They Carried*, "The Lives of the Dead." In that story, Tim the narrator directly and positively relates the death of his childhood friend Linda to the deaths of his fellow soldiers. His response in both cases is identical: he daydreams about them and tries to preserve them with stories. The death of Linda demonstrates O'Brien's efforts to achieve a moment of *communitas* with his readers beyond the confines of the text. By ending with a story about coping with a little girl's death from circumstances beyond her control, O'Brien reaches out to readers who never went to war. Anyone can relate to Timmy's grief and response to Linda's death; thus anyone should be able to relate to Tim's grief and response to the deaths of his fellow soldiers. Communicating the war experience in a meaningful way to people who have never been in combat is O'Brien's primary purpose. O'Brien's joy as a writer derives from his touching those who haven't lived what he has lived (e.g., McNerney 24–25).

The Things They Carried thus achieves—at the very least aspires to achieve—the *communitas* of pilgrimage among the soldiers in the unit, between the narrator-character and the enemy, and between the narrator-character, author, and the reader. If this novel's narrative journey holds any promise of redemption, it would be in whether it succeeds in meeting O'Brien's moral imperative of imaginative identification, the moral imperative that just might prevent the next bad war from ever occurring. Yet, for Tim the narrator and O'Brien the author, we still must ask whether this communication of the war experience to others is sufficient for quieting his own demons, for alleviating his spiritual turmoil. Is this novel's pilgrimage a success for its narrator and its author?

* * *

If "at the end of a story you feel uplifted," the narrator of "How to Tell a True War Story" argues, "or if you feel that some small bit of rectitude has been salvaged from the larger waste, then you have been made the victim of a very old and terrible lie" (69). Here is the way the book ends, with the story "The Lives of the Dead," narrated by Tim:

> And then it becomes 1990. I'm forty-three years old, and a writer now, still dreaming Linda alive in exactly the same way. She's not

the embodied Linda; she's mostly made up, with a new identity and a new name, like the man who never was. Her real name doesn't matter. She was nine years old. I loved her and she died. And yet right here, in the spell of memory and imagination, I can still see her as if through ice, as if I'm gazing into some other world, a place where there are no brain tumors and no funeral homes, where there are no bodies at all. I can see Kiowa, too, and Ted Lavender and Curt Lemon, and sometimes I can even see Timmy skating with Linda under the yellow floodlights. I'm young and happy. I'll never die. I'm skimming across the surface of my own history, moving fast, riding the melt beneath the blades, doing loops and spins, and when I take a high leap into the dark and come down thirty years later, I realize it is as Tim trying to save Timmy's life with a story. (245–46)

Can imagination save us, uplift us, provide some small bit of rectitude, if only temporarily, or is it the very perpetrator of that old and terrible lie? The lie, of course, is the illusion of meaning, of spiritual gain, of recovery of innocence, in the act of creating or receiving a war story.

Metaphorically, Linda's death during Timmy's childhood in the collection's final story can be viewed as Tim's loss of innocence in Vietnam, and in this way it connects with his obsessive insistence on Martha's virginity in the book's first and title story—as truly an obsessive clinging to his own innocence and a refusal to acknowledge its loss in Vietnam. Concluding this novel with the childhood memory returns the veteran to his pre-war self, as so many veteran narratives try to do, but it also knows the impossibility of such a return. Even the death of a little girl can't but be seen through the lens of the war experience. The possible achievement of *communitas* notwithstanding, the prospect of saving Timmy's life with a story, the possibility of Tim's complete moral cleansing and his return to the innocence of his youthful pre-war self, strikes me as bleak. Tim wants desperately to believe in the power of the imagination to save Timmy's life by leaping high and landing on some epiphany or understanding or enlightenment, but eventually imagination's "high leap in the dark" comes to an end, and it is thirty years later: the dead are still dead, we cannot believe that Curt Lemon's final thoughts were of sunlight, and Tim and O'Brien are neither young nor happy.

O'Brien's other work provides context for the bleakness belying the hope in the transforming power of story-truth in *The Things They Carried*. The role call of the dead that begins both his early Vietnam novels, *Going after Cacciato* and *The Things They Carried*, has an echo in "The Violent Vet," his early non-fiction piece from 1979: "Out of more than 2.5 million men who actually served in Southeast Asia, some 57,000 died and another 300,000 were wounded, 150,000 of them seriously enough to require hospitalization. Of those wounded, some 75,000 came home with serious handicaps, while about 25,000 returned totally disabled; 5,283 men came home with one missing limb; 61 came home as triple amputees" (103). And in "The Vietnam in Me," O'Brien tells us about being shown scars on the bodies of Vietnamese women and "what's left of a man named Nguyen Van Ngu. They balance this wreckage on a low chair. Both legs are gone at the upper-upper thigh" (56). The references to scars and amputees are especially telling. It's easy enough to re-animate the non-present dead through the imagination. It's impossible to restore a limb imaginatively to a person sitting in front of you.

Northern Lights, O'Brien's first novel, treats apocalypse "as the startling fact of modern life," as he told Larry McCaffrey in an interview (141). His third novel, *The Nuclear Age*, explores one man's response to the threat of nuclear apocalypse as a metaphor for the man's fear of both his own death and the death of all things, "not only human mortality," O'Brien says, "but the mortality of the universe as well: the sun is going to flare up and roast the earth and then die out" (qtd. in McNerney 11). As an adult, the novel's protagonist, William Cowling, imagines the end of it all. "In the attic, a warhead no doubt burns. Everything is combustible. Faith burns. Trust burns. Everything burns to nothing and even nothing burns. [...] And when there is nothing, there is nothing worth dying for and when there is nothing worth dying for, there is only nothing" (*Nuclear* 303). As a twelve-year-old boy in the 1950s, Cowling protected himself from radioactive fallout by hoarding lead pencils in his basement Ping-Pong-table bomb shelter—as if pencils could ever save anyone, O'Brien the writer included. O'Brien's spiritual metaphor of salvation through storytelling, against such an apocalyptic and secular outlook, seems based upon an empty hope. The power of language to mollify the soul's pain is a trick, an illusion, like O'Brien's repeated insistence in several works that by changing the language of death he and his fellow soldiers could make it less real: "It's easier to cope with a kicked bucket than a corpse; if it isn't human, it doesn't matter much if it's dead" (238).

Because in the end O'Brien doesn't trust language. In 1994, during his return trip to Vietnam, O'Brien stands in front of a ditch at My Lai, "where maybe 50, maybe 80, maybe 100 innocent human beings perished." He focusses on the facts: 504 dead—"women, infants, teenagers, old men"—in an area that saw civilian casualties "approaching 50,000 a year" (52). Words fail him. Words can't express the misery, words can't make a difference: "I want a miracle. That's the final emotion. The terror at this ditch, the certain doom, the need for God's intervention," and the unstated fear that it will never come ("Vietnam" 53). O'Brien's response, the response of the woman with him, the response of the

Vietnamese survivors with him, is silence. Language can do nothing. It cannot adequately express, it cannot change the facts, it cannot redeem anything. There is no saving of these dead souls, or of anyone's living soul. As crucial and powerful as imagination and language are, O'Brien's writing, in the end, reveals their limitations. Like the childhood magic tricks to which he compares his writing, "what seemed to happen became a happening in itself" only "for a time. [. . .] It was an illusion, of course—the creating of a new and improved reality" ("Magic" 175). At the end of the private show, one must come up from the basement and face the world. We all leave the show knowing that none of it was real, knowing that none of it meant anything at all.

Revisiting Vietnam in his memory has sent O'Brien to the edge of suicide, yet he has gone back, seeking always somehow "to save Timmy's life with a story." That he has kept going back, that he has circled around that part of his life like Norman Bowker circling the lake, suggests the success of each narrative pilgrimage. "You can tell a true war story," O'Brien tells us, "if you just keep on telling it" (*Things* 85). As I think "The Vietnam in Me" expresses, the more O'Brien has gone back, the more he has realized the futility of finding redemptive dignity or moral grounding. He can't save himself, or Kiowa, or O'Brien's real buddy Chip. The actual site of his journey, the war in Vietnam, holds no solid moral framework, religious or political, upon which he can hang his individual value system. "In a destabilized system," Turner and Turner write, "life has become one long pilgrimage, without map or sacred goal" (237). O'Brien's problem, then, has been that his narrative pilgrimages have lacked the necessary institutionalized and internalized sources of meaning.

Somehow, however, O'Brien has survived. The years around 1994, the year of "The Vietnam in Me" and his darkest novel, *In the Lake of the Woods*, were by all accounts his personal nadir. His two novels since that period, *Tomcat in Love* and *July, July*, show a marked turn of spirits. *Tomcat in Love* is a comedy that pokes fun at—among other things—a Vietnam veteran, Thomas Chippering, with an exaggerated paranoia of the ghosts of his wartime past and with a habit of spinning language to deceive himself. "Although the [Vietnam] war is uncovered as a traumatic experience for Chippering," Heberle writes, "his own self-representation, his unreliability as a narrator, and even the persuasiveness of his traumatization subvert the conventional solemnity of the subject" (*Lake* 282). Thus O'Brien uses the novel to parody himself, both his endless writing on the subject of Vietnam, on his chaotic love life, and on the relation between the two, as he pokes fun of his mantra from "The Vietnam in Me" or that his "inexhaustible need for affection" and love has led him to war and other inexcusable acts (*Tomcat* 158). After the emotional nightmare of writing *In the Lake of the Woods*, writing *Tomcat in Love* helped O'Brien recover by permitting him to laugh at himself and "lighten up a bit." The result, in Heberle's estimation, is "his most original revision of his previous work and of himself" (289).

In *July, July*, O'Brien for the first time has imagined a character able to escape the war. Billy McMann flees to Canada and, at his high school reunion thirty-one years later, begins a new future with a woman who just happens to be a former minister. The other characters in the novel also have arrived at contentment, and, despite the class reunion as the frame story, the novel looks forward, propelling the reader and the characters to whatever happens after the last page, instead of back into the past, back into the book, into the war, as the earlier novels did. We might speculate that O'Brien has realized the futility of transcending war's meaningless through writing and has relieved himself of the burden of salvaging any personal meaning from his Vietnam experiences beyond the simple act of sharing them with others. Which he has already done several times. Relieved of the past, his writing has begun to imagine the future.

WORKS CITED

Bates, Milton J. *The Wars We Took to Vietnam: Cultural Conflict and Storytelling*. Berkeley: U of California P, 1996.

Bunyan, John. *The Pilgrim's Progress*. 1907. Intro. and notes by G. B. Harrison. Everyman's Library. New York: E.P. Dutton, 1954.

cummings, e.e. *The Enormous Room*. 1922. Ed. and intro. Samuel Hynes. Penguin Twentieth-Century Classics. New York: Penguin, 1999.

Dunn, Maggie, and Ann Morris. *The Composite Novel: The Short Story Cycle in Transition*. New York: Twayne, 1995.

Eakin, Paul John. *How Our Lives Become Stories: Making Selves*. Ithaca, NY: Cornell UP, 1999.

Fussell, Paul. *The Great War and Modern Memory*. London: Oxford UP, 1975.

Heberle, Mark A. *A Trauma Artist: Tim O'Brien and the Fiction of Vietnam*. Iowa City: U of Iowa P, 2001.

Leed, Eric J. *No Man's Land: Combat and Identity in World War I*. Cambridge, UK: Cambridge UP, 1979.

McCaffery, Larry. Interview with Tim O'Brien. *Chicago Review* 33.2 (1982): 129–49.

McNerney, Brian C. "Responsibly Inventing History: An Interview with Tim O'Brien." *War, Literature, & the Arts* 6.2 (Fall–Winter 1994): 1–26.

Naparsteck, Martin. Interview with Tim O'Brien. *Contemporary Literature* 32.1 (Spring 1991): 1–11.

O'Brien, Tim. *Going after Cacciato*. New York: Broadway Books, 1978.

———. *If I Die in a Combat Zone, Box Me Up and Ship Me Home*. New York: Broadway Books, 1973.

———. *In the Lake of the Woods*. New York: Penguin, 1994.

———. *July, July*. Boston: Houghton Mifflin, 2002.

———. "The Magic Show." *Writers on Writing*. Ed. Robert Pack and Jay Parini. Hanover, NH: UP of New England, 1991. 175–83.

———. *Northern Lights*. New York: Broadway Books, 1975.

———. *The Nuclear Age*. New York: Penguin Books, 1985.

———. *The Things They Carried*. New York: Broadway Books, 1990.

———. *Tomcat in Love*. New York: Broadway Books, 1998.

———. "The Vietnam in Me." *New York Times Magazine* (2 October 1994): 48–57.

———. "The Violent Vet." *Esquire* (December 1979): 96–97, 99–100, 103–04.

O'Gorman, Farrell. "The Things They Carried as Composite Novel." *War, Literature & the Arts* 10.2 (Fall–Winter 1998): 289–309.

Turner, Victor. "Pilgrimages as Social Processes." *Dramas, Fields, and Metaphors*. Ithaca, NY: Cornell UP, 1974.

Turner, Victor, and Edith Turner. *Image and Pilgrimage in Christian Culture: Anthropological Perspectives*. New York: Columbia UP, 1978.

Vonnegut, Kurt, Jr. *Slaughterhouse-Five*. New York: Dell, 1969.

Chronology

1946   Born William Timothy O'Brien Jr. on October 1 in Austin, Minnesota. Father is William T. O'Brien, Sr., an insurance salesman; mother is Ava E. Schultz O'Brien, an elementary school teacher.

1956   Family moves to Worthington, Minnesota.

1964   Attends Macalester College in St. Paul, Minnesota.

1967   Studies in Prague in summer; writes novel as course project.

1968   Graduates summa cum laude and Phi Beta Kappa from Macalester. In August, drafted into the U.S. Army.

1969–70   Serves in Vietnam. Awarded Purple Heart.

1970–76   Ph.D. student in government at Harvard University; passes orals and completes part of dissertation; leaves to become full-time writer.

1971–72   Interns at *Washington Post* during summers.

1973–74   During leave of absence from Harvard, works as general assignment reporter on national affairs desk at *Washington Post*.

1973   Publishes *If I Die in a Combat Zone*. Marries Ann Weller, an editorial assistant at Little, Brown publishing company.

1975   Publishes *Northern Lights*.

1976	Wins O. Henry Memorial Award for an excerpt from *Going After Cacciato*.
1978	Publishes *Going After Cacciato*, and short story "Speaking of Courage" wins O. Henry Award.
1978–79	Writer in residence at Emerson College, Boston, Massachusetts.
1979	*Going After Cacciato* wins National Book Award.
1985	Publishes *The Nuclear Age*.
1989	Short story "The Things They Carried" wins National Magazine Award in Fiction.
1990	Publishes *The Things They Carried*. Finalist for Pulitzer Prize and National Book Critics Circle Award.
1994	Returns to Vietnam for first time since tour of duty. Publishes *In the Lake of the Woods*, named by *Time* magazine as best work of fiction published in 1994.
1995	Divorces wife after long separation.
1998	Publishes *Tomcat in Love*.
1999–	Assumes position of Roy F. and Joann Mitte Chair in Creative Writing at Texas State University–San Marcos.
2001	Marries Meredith Hale Baker, professional actor/director who teaches in the theater department at Texas State University.
2002	*July, July* published.
2003	First son born. "What Went Wrong" from *July, July* selected for O. Henry Award.
2005	Second son born.

Contributors

HAROLD BLOOM is Sterling Professor of the Humanities at Yale University. Educated at Cornell and Yale universities, he is the author of more than 30 books, including *Shelley's Mythmaking* (1959), *The Visionary Company* (1961), *Blake's Apocalypse* (1963), *Yeats* (1970), *The Anxiety of Influence* (1973), *A Map of Misreading* (1975), *Kabbalah and Criticism* (1975), *Agon: Toward a Theory of Revisionism* (1982), *The American Religion* (1992), *The Western Canon* (1994), *Omens of Millennium: The Gnosis of Angels, Dreams, and Resurrection* (1996), *Shakespeare: The Invention of the Human* (1998), *How to Read and Why* (2000), *Genius: A Mosaic of One Hundred Exemplary Creative Minds* (2002), *Hamlet: Poem Unlimited* (2003), *Where Shall Wisdom Be Found?* (2004), and *Jesus and Yahweh: The Names Divine* (2005). In addition, he is the author of hundreds of articles, reviews, and editorial introductions. In 1999, Professor Bloom received the American Academy of Arts and Letters' Gold Medal for Criticism. He has also received the International Prize of Catalonia, the Alfonso Reyes Prize of Mexico, and the Hans Christian Andersen Bicentennial Prize of Denmark.

FARRELL O'GORMAN is an associate professor in the Catholic studies department at DePaul University, and the author of *Peculiar Crossroads: Flannery O'Connor, Walker Percy, and Catholic Vision in Postwar Southern Fiction* and a novel.

MATS TEGMARK is a senior lecturer in literature at the Dalarna University Centre for Irish Studies at Högskolan Dalarna, Sweden.

DAVID R. JARRAWAY is a professor at the University of Ottawa. His work includes *Wallace Stevens and the Question of Belief: "Metaphysician in the*

Dark" and *"Going the Distance": Dissident Subjectivity in Modernist American Literature.*

JIM NEILSON has been an instructor in the department of arts and sciences at Trident Technical College. He is coeditor of *World Views—Classic and Contemporary Readings* and has contributed to publications.

CARL S. HORNER is a professor at Flagler College, St. Augustine, Florida. He has published *The Boy inside the American Businessman: Corporate Darwinism in Twentieth-Century American Literature.* He also has published poetry, articles, and book reviews.

CHRISTOPHER MICHAEL MCDONOUGH is an associate professor of classical languages at Sewanee: The University of the South. He coauthored an annotated translation of *Servius' Commentary on Book Four of Virgil's Aeneid.* He also has authored scholarly articles.

PAMELA SMILEY is a professor and chair of the English department at Carthage College in Wisconsin. She has conducted extensive research work in literature and composition, expository writing, creative writing, and women's studies.

SUSAN FARRELL is a professor at the College of Charleston. She is working on a book on Tim O'Brien and has published *Critical Companion to Kurt Vonnegut: A Literary Reference to His Life and Work.*

ALEX VERNON is an associate professor at Hendrix College in Conway, Arkansas. He has published *Soldiers Once and Still: Ernest Hemingway, James Salter, and Tim O'Brien* and other work, and he is the editor of *Arms & the Self: War, the Military, and Autobiographical Writing.*

Bibliography

Beidler, Philip D. *Re-Writing America: Vietnam Authors in Their Generation*. Athens: University of Georgia Press, 1991.

Caulfield, Peter. "Vietnam Voices; or, Uncle Ho Meets Country Joe (and the Fish)." *Writing on the Edge* 11, no. 2 (Spring–Summer 2000): 21–32.

Chen, Tina. "'Unraveling the Deeper Meaning': Exile and the Embodied Poetics of Displacement in Tim O'Brien's *The Things They Carried*." *Contemporary Literature* 39, no. 1 (Spring 1998): 77–98.

Daley, Chris. "The 'Atrocious Privilege': Bearing Witness to War and Atrocity in O'Brien, Levi, and Remarque." In *Arms and the Self: War, the Military, and Autobiographical Writing*, edited by Alex Vernon, pp. 182–201. Kent, Ohio: Kent State University Press, 2005.

Donovan, Christopher. *Postmodern Counternarratives: Irony and Audience in the Novels of Paul Auster, Don DeLillo, Charles Johnson, and Tim O'Brien*. New York: Routledge, 2005.

Dunnaway, Jen. "Approaching a Truer Form of Truth: The Appropriation of the Oral Narrative Form in Vietnam War Literature." In *Soldier Talk: The Vietnam War in Oral Narrative*, edited by Paul Budra and Michael Zeitlin, pp. 26–51. Bloomington: Indiana University Press, 2004.

———. "'One More Redskin Bites the Dirt': Racial Melancholy in Vietnam War Representation." *Arizona Quarterly: A Journal of American Literature, Culture, and Theory* 64, no. 1 (Spring 2008): 109–29.

Gilmore, Barry, and Alexander Kaplan. *Tim O'Brien in the Classroom: "This Too Is True: Stories Can Save Us."* Urbana, Ill.: National Council of Teachers of English, 2007.

Heberle, Mark A. *A Trauma Artist: Tim O'Brien and the Fiction of Vietnam*. Iowa City: University of Iowa Press, 2001.

Herzog, Tobey C. *Tim O'Brien*. New York: Twayne Publishers; London: Prentice Hall International, 1997.

———. *Writing Vietnam, Writing Life: Caputo, Heinemann, O'Brien, Butler*. Iowa City: University of Iowa Press, 2008.

Hicks, Patrick. "A Conversation with Tim O'Brien." *Indiana Review* 27, no. 2 (Winter 2005): 85–95.

Juncker, Clara. "Not a Story to Pass On? Tim O'Brien's Vietnam." In *Transnational America: Contours of Modern US Culture*, edited by Russell Duncan and Clara Juncker, pp. 111–24. Copenhagen, Denmark: Museum Tusculanum; 2004.

Kaplan, Steven. *Understanding Tim O'Brien*. Columbia: University of South Carolina Press, 1995.

Kazemek, Francis E. "*The Things They Carried*: Vietnam War Literature by and about Women in the Secondary Classroom." *Journal of Adolescent and Adult Literacy* 42, no. 3 (November 1998): 156–65.

Lustig, T. J. "'Moments of Punctuation': Metonymy and Ellipsis in Tim O'Brien." *Yearbook of English Studies* 31 (2001): 74–92.

McCay, Mary A. "The Autobiography of Guilt: Tim O'Brien and Vietnam." In *Writing Lives: American Biography and Autobiography*, edited by Hans Bak and Hans Krabbendam, pp. 115–21. Amsterdam, Netherlands: VU UP, 1998.

Naparsteck, Martin. "An Interview with Tim O'Brien." *Contemporary Literature* 32 (Spring 1991): 1–11.

Pasternak, Donna. "Keeping the Dead Alive: Revising the Past in Tim O'Brien's War Stories." *Irish Journal of American Studies* 7 (1998): 41–54.

Renny, Christopher. *The Viet Nam War, The American War*. Amherst: University of Massachusetts Press, 1995.

Seung, Ah Oh. "Women in Vietnam War Literature and the Discourse of Heteronormative Domesticity: Tim O'Brien and Erica Jong." *Feminist Studies in English Literature* 16, no. 1 (Summer 2008): 71–90.

Shostak, Debra. "Artful Dodge Interviews Tim O'Brien." *The Artful Dodge* 17 (1991): 74–90.

Silbergleid, Robin. "Making Things Present: Tim O'Brien's Autobiographical Metafiction." *Contemporary Literature* 50, no. 1 (Spring 2009): 129–55.

Smith, Patrick A. *Tim O'Brien: A Critical Companion*. Westport, Conn.: Greenwood Press, 2005.

Taft-Kaufman, Jill. "How to Tell a True War Story: The Dramaturgy and Staging of Narrative Theatre." *Theatre Topics* 10, no. 1 (March 2000): 17–38.

Taylor, Mark. "Tim O'Brien's War." *The Centennial Review* 39, no. 2 (Spring 1995): 213–30.

Tischler, Nancy M. *Encyclopedia of Contemporary Christian Fiction: From C.S. Lewis to Left Behind*. Santa Barbara, Calif.: Greenwood Press, 2009.

Tran, Jonathan. "Emplotting Forgiveness: Narrative, Forgetting and Memory." *Literature & Theology: An International Journal of Religion, Theory, and Culture* 23, no. 2 (June 2009): 220–33.

Vernon, Alex. *Soldiers Once and Still: Ernest Hemingway, James Salter, and Tim O'Brien*. Iowa City: University of Iowa Press, 2004.

Wesley, Marilyn C. "Young Goodmen at War: Thom Jones's *The Pugilist at Rest* and Tim O'Brien's *The Things They Carried*." In *Violent Adventure: Contemporary Fiction by American Men*. Charlottesville: University of Virginia Press, 2003.

Wharton, Lynn. "Tim O'Brien and American National Identity: A Vietnam Veteran's Imagined Self in *The Things They Carried*." *49th Parallel: An Interdisciplinary Journal of North American Studies* 5 (Spring 2000): (no pagination).

Acknowledgments

Farrell O'Gorman, "*The Things They Carried* as Composite Novel." From *War, Literature, and the Arts* 10, no. 2 (Fall-Winter 1998): 289–309. Copyright © 1998 Farrell O'Gorman.

Tegmark Mats. "The Perspectives of Other Characters." From *In the Shoes of a Soldier: Communication in Tim O'Brien's Vietnam Narratives*, pp. 245–71. Published by Uppsala University. Copyright © 1998 Mats Tegmark.

David R. Jarraway, "'Excremental Assault' in Tim O'Brien: Trauma and Recovery in Vietnam War Literature." From *Modern Fiction Studies* 44, no. 3 (Fall 1998): 695–711. Copyright © 1998 by the Purdue Research Foundation.

Jim Neilson, "Undying Uncertainty." From *Warring Fictions: American Literary Culture and the Vietnam War Narrative*, pp. 192–209. Copyright © 1998 by University Press of Mississippi.

Carl S. Horner, "Challenging the Law of Courage and Heroic Identification in Tim O'Brien's *If I Die in a Combat Zone* and *The Things They Carried*." From *War, Literature, and the Arts* 11, no. 1 (Spring-Summer 1999): 256–67. Copyright © 1999 Carl S. Horner.

Christopher Michael McDonough, "'Afraid to Admit We Are Not Achilles': Facing Hector's Dilemma in Tim O'Brien's *The Things They Carried*." From *Classical and Modern Literature* 20, no. 3 (Spring 2000): 23–32. Copyright © 2000 Classical and Modern Literature, Inc.

Pamela Smiley, "The Role of the Ideal (Female) Reader in Tim O'Brien's *The Things They Carried*: Why Should Real Women Play?" From *The Massachusetts Review* 43, no. 4 (Winter 2002-2003): 602–13. Copyright © 2003 *The Massachusetts Review*.

Susan Farrell, "Tim O'Brien and Gender: A Defense of *The Things They Carried*." From *The CEA Critic* 66, no. 1 (Fall 2003): 1–21. Copyright © 2003 by the College English Association.

Alex Vernon, "Salvation, Storytelling, and Pilgrimage in Tim O'Brien *The Things They Carried*." From *Mosaic* 36, no. 4 (December 2003): 171–88. Copyright © 2003 *Mosaic*.

Index

Characters in literary works are indexed by first name (if any), followed by the name of the work in parentheses